Texas Banker/ Oklahoma Hunter

(A Mostly True Story)

By Ken Mixon

Illustrated by Richard Stubler

Ken Mixon, 1112 Deep Water Cove, Corsicana, Texas 75109

International Standard Book Number: 978-0-692-76098-7

Contents

Dedication

My wife, Carol Mixon, is a incredible partner and marrying her was the best decision of my life. She has always tolerated all the time I spend hunting and fishing and is probably relieved sometimes when I leave for another trip. I have a wonderful daughter, Beth Killian and a fantastic son, Drew Mixon. This book is dedicated to Carol, Beth and Drew.

I want to say a special thank you to my great friend Larry Miller. He has helped me run banks since 2001 and was kind enough to proof read this for me. Thank you, Larry.

My good friend Dr. Jody Tacker did the final edit. Thank you, Jody.

These stories are mostly true. I have changed the names, details, and dates to protect the innocent as well as the guilty.

As a thank you for buying the book, I am including my "famous" Chili recipe – no additional charge.

Oklahoma Son Chili

Take 1/2 pound very lean ground beef.

Take ½ pound pork sausage.

Fry until brown. (Cast iron skillet if possible)

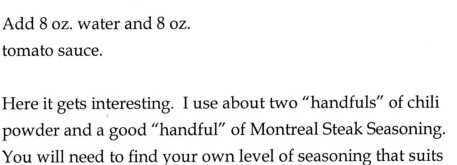

Drain all grease off. (Very important!)

Place back into large skillet.

Add 8 oz. water and 8 oz. tomato sauce.

Here it gets interesting. I use about two "handfuls" of chili powder and a good "handful" of Montreal Steak Seasoning. You will need to find your own level of seasoning that suits you.

Simmer 1 hour or so at low heat.

Feeds 3 to 4.

If you add beans to this chili, I will lose my mind. But, go ahead if you want to.

Chapter 1

Starting Out

I started out my career, some forty years ago, in bank operations in the late seventies. I was a bank auditor for about six
months, traveling the state of Oklahoma auditing banks until
I took a position with a small bank in eastern Oklahoma near
Fort Smith, Arkansas.

I remember my first day. I came in, was introduced to the
bank staff, and then trained with a teller for the day. At the
end of the first day, the bank president told the Cashier that,
"Ken has trained enough, we are paying him $700 a month,
put him in a teller window and turn him loose."

I had a college degree and six months banking experience. I was as green as green could be. But the bank president did not want to waste any time getting me productive since, in his mind, they were paying me the princely sum of $4.04 per hour.

The first day in the teller window, I struggled. I had handled cash in the past but it is an entirely different thing when you are doing just that all day long. I was unfamiliar with their procedures and I did not know the customers. At the end of the day I had to count up my cash and balance my window. I counted my cash, went through the process, and discovered I was short $100. I could not believe it.

Wanda, the head teller, came over and checked over my work. I was short $100, no doubt about it.

In a little bit, the president of the bank called me into his office. He said, "Ken, we like you and are happy you are here. I think that you will have a long career in banking. But if you lose another #$@ nickel, I am going to fire you."

I was sick to my stomach. My wife and I had only been married six months and we had just moved 150 miles to this community.

The next day, I walked into the bank and went straight to Wanda. Wanda had worked for the bank for fifteen years and was a great teller and a great person. "Wanda," I said, "I need your help in the worst way." I told her what the president had told me and, God bless her, she took pity on me. She trained me for the next four hours and when she was finished I had it all down. I made it through that day and the following years being a teller only due to her training.

I never lost another nickel while I was a teller. I was also probably the slowest teller in the state of Oklahoma. I would count money three times before I ever finished a transaction. That does not sound bad, but you have to consider that we would have business owners who would bring in thousands of dollars in ones, fives, tens, and twenties to make a deposit in those days. Most people either paid in cash or check. There were very few credit card transactions in those days and debit cards did not yet exist.

Later, about 1989, I was working at a chain of banks in Texas called First City. I had been promoted to president of First City Bank of Garland. One of my friends, who I will call Gary, was promoted to president of another First City bank location. Gary, unlike me, had no experience in operations and had only been on the lending side of the bank. Like many loan officers today, he had started as a credit analyst, writing up loan packages for the loan committee before he became a loan officer. Gary was a great guy, but he was not ready to run a bank when this opportunity came along. He was calling me about once a week to get my opinion on issues on both lending and operations.

Six months after becoming president, Gary had a new client come into his bank and open an account. Gary met the two owners of FGH Company and was impressed with them. A couple of months passed. One of the owners of FGH came into Gary's bank and deposited a check for $124,000. The teller took the check to Gary and he gave them immediate credit for the funds.

Although customers do not usually realize it, there can be an element of risk when a bank accepts a check for deposit. The bank expects the check to "clear," which means that the bank the check is drawn on will pay the funds to the bank. If the check "bounces," the bank must recover the money. The operations staff of a bank has to continually make decisions on which checks will clear and which may not.

In this case, the check did not clear. In a week, the check was returned to the bank as insufficient funds. Gary called the owners of FGH in to his office and told the owners that they had to come up with $124,000 to cover their now overdrawn account. The owners told Gary that they had received this money from an investor and that they had no reason to believe that the check was not good. They had spent this money on their business and did not have $124,000 to give to the bank. Weeks passed, the owners did not come up with any money and their account remained overdrawn.

Gary's superiors at First City became aware of the situation. After due review, Gary was terminated. Gary had made a decision that cost the bank $124,000. The customer was new to the bank and Gary should have been more cautious in accepting checks for deposits. He did not have the training he needed to do his job.

I felt bad for Gary, but I understood. I have always been proud that I began my career as a teller. Over the years at different banking jobs, I got a great banking education. This was primarily due to people like Wanda and others who helped this young man from Oklahoma begin his banking career. God bless them all. Thank you, Wanda, Don Barnard, and the many other mentors I have had. I have tried to pass along what you taught me to others as I have worked in banking.

One of the most important things I learned early in my banking career is that I am only as good as the people I work with each day. Over the years, I have worked with some tremendous bankers. There are too many to list all of them here but some of the very best were Larry Miller, Chris Story, Trish Bienvenu, Laura Vidaurri, Kofi Asante, Mark Jordan, Tammie Perry, and Donna Miller. I also have many terrific customers, many of whom have become great friends. Frankly, without the support of these people and others, I would have had little success in my banking career. Thank you all.

Chapter 2

Fireworks

I just loved fireworks when I was a kid. My family did not have a lot of money while I was growing up, but Dad always let me have a little money for the Fourth of July. I would buy Roman candles, bottle rockets, smoke bombs, and Black Cat firecrackers.

It is hard to believe today, but back when I was about ten, our parents would allow us to handle fireworks with no adult supervision. It was a different time. The neighborhood boys would find someplace outside of town and have fireworks wars. We would shoot bottle rockets and Roman candles at each other and then pitch firecrackers at each other. It was great fun but dangerous, now that I look back on it. One kid got a Roman candle ball stuck in his shirt and it burned him a little. We were lucky no one got seriously injured.

The summer I was eleven, a friend and I rode our bikes down to the rodeo grounds which were about a half mile from my house. The rodeo grounds had been there for years and the stands and fencing were made from wood. Through the years in the sun, the wood had become quite dry. The entrance to the rodeo grounds had a six foot fence that ran parallel to the road for about fifty yards. My friend Ricky and I were pitching Black Cats and bottle rockets over the fence. We were playing as if we had grenades and were throwing them over the fence to kill the bad guys.

After we had been doing this for thirty minutes, Ricky turned to me and asked, "Do you smell something burning?" I laughed and said, "Of course I smell something burning, we have firecrackers!"

Ricky said, "No, I am not talking about that. I smell something else."

I climbed up so I could see over the fence. It had been a very dry summer that year and as I looked over the fence, I could see that the grass was on fire and was spreading quickly. This presented a real problem. My father was a volunteer firefighter in my hometown and he would be none too pleased to hear that I had been part of setting a field on fire. So we did what any eleven year old boys would do, we got on our bikes and flew out of there so fast that our wheels were barely touching the pavement.

The wind was blowing just right that day to blow that grass fire right into the rodeo grounds. Once the fire hit the wooden stands and wooden fencing, there was no chance the local firefighters could put it out. The stands and fencing burned like they were soaked with kerosene. In the end, they burned completely to the ground.

Some of you may wonder if I ever told my father that we caused that fire. I am proud to tell you that I did. Of course I was fifty when I told him, but I finally did mention it.

Surprisingly after that incident I decided the next summer that I was going to make one big bomb. My folks both worked all year round, so I was pretty much free in the summer to do boy things. I spent hours carefully taking the powder out of three hundred Black Cat firecrackers. Then, I took the powder out of one hundred bottle rockets for good measure. When this was complete, I had a good handful of powder in a Mason jar.

Since the rodeo grounds were gone, I had a dilemma on my hands. Where could I set off the bomb? I finally decided to ride my bike to the ball park and set it off from the pitcher's mound. (I cannot explain my reasoning; it just made sense to me at the time.) I rode my bike to the ball park which was about a mile from my house. I carefully poured the powder in a big pile at the pitcher's mound. I was expecting a big boom so I was a little nervous about lighting the pile. I did not have a fuse so I was just throwing lit matches at the pile. I kept missing the pile.

Finally after ten attempts, I got a little closer and dropped a lit match on the pile of powder. It did not explode but rather flashed very brightly. I was very interested in what was going to happen so I was watching closely. (Kids, do not try this!) I was completely blinded by the flash. All I could see was a bright spot. I started crying and believed that I had blinded myself for life. I crawled over to the dugout and cried for thirty minutes. How was I going to get home? How could I tell my parents what I had done? My father would kill me.

Finally, I began to be able to see a little bit out of the corners of my eyes. I jumped on my bike and rode home. I am happy to say that my sight fully recovered in a couple of hours.

Thus ended my bomb making days.

Chapter 3

Intro to Texas Banking

In the early 1980s, I was working for a bank in Dallas. Their loan committee process was completely different from any that I had seen up to that time. At most banks, loans above a certain dollar figure (like $300,000) go to a group of senior bankers for approval. The thought is that this group hopefully has the wisdom and experience to decide whether a loan is a good risk for the bank for the return therein.

At this particular bank, the Senior Loan Officer was signing off on the bigger loans and then the loan was booked. Once a month, everyone in the bank who was involved in lending, from loan assistants to loan processing clerks to the loan officers and senior officers would meet in one big room. Then, the front sheet of the each loan write-up would be projected on a wall and the lending officer would discuss the loan. He or she would talk about the borrower and the collateral and we would go on to the next loan. At the end of the meeting, we had, in effect, approved the loans and went on about our business.

Obviously, in this method, there was no real analysis of the loan. So, after I had been there a while, I approached the president of the bank and proposed that we form a real loan committee of four to six officers to properly discuss the loan proposals, analyze the risk, and make better credit decisions. After about a month, we put a real loan committee in place. In the third month, our Senior Vice President of Commercial Real Estate lending brought in a loan. For my purposes, I will call him Mark. Mark presented his loan. The borrower owned a business and was buying a piece of land next to his business for future expansion. Here are the details of the loan.

Purchase price: $800,000

Appraised value: $1,400,000 (more on this later)

Loan amount: $1,100,000

I was much younger and less experienced then than I am now so it did not jump out at me why a property was appraising for $1,400,000 that had a sales price of $800,000. But I did not understand why the bank would loan $1,100,000 on the property if the borrower was only paying $800,000 for the property.

So I asked Mark, "Why are we lending this guy $1,100,000 on a property that he is buying for $800,000?"

Mark: "He is getting one heck of a buy on this. It has been listed at $1,400,000, but the seller really needs cash so the seller is letting it go at a steal."

Me: "Ok, the borrower is getting a great deal. Why are we lending him $300,000 over the purchase price?"

Mark: "If you look at his business financials, he needs capital for his expanding business. So we are lending him the $300,000 to help expand his business. If you will notice, we are only lending him 78% of appraised value."

*Sidenote. The bank already had made a loan to the borrower for working capital for his business, but I was too inexperienced a banker at this point to realize this.

Me: "Look, Mark, I have not been a Texas banker for that long, but in Oklahoma banking where I was trained, we would loan the lower of 80% of purchase price or 80% of appraisal. That would mean our loan would be for $640,000 not $1,100,000. That would also mean our borrower has some skin in the game (equity)."

Mark had not been used to anyone really questioning him on his loans, other than the Senior Loan Officer. This borrower had over $1,000,000 in deposits and $3,000,000 in loans in the bank already, so he was pretty displeased to have to defend this loan, particularly to an officer who was a lower officer in the bank than he was.

Mark, raising his voice, "Alright Mixon! Let's do the math on this. Let's compare your proposed loan with my proposed loan. Your proposed loan on this deal is at $640,000 with a fee to the bank of $6,400 (1%) and the loan rate is 10%. My proposed loan on this deal is $1,100,000 with a fee of $11,000 and the loan rate is 10%. Which loan will make more money for the bank?!"

I was dumbfounded. I looked around at the rest of the committee and saw that everyone at the table agreed with Mark. I voted no. Everyone else voted yes and the loan passed. (My nickname became Dr. No for this vote and other no votes later.) That was when I knew that Texas banking was very different than what I was used to in Oklahoma.

The question of the borrower having equity in the purchase was overruled so the bank could make a larger fee and make more interest over the life of the loan (assuming the loan paid in full).

Eighteen months later, the borrower quit paying on the loan and the bank foreclosed on the property. Even I was surprised when I found out the bank finally sold the property for only $475,000, taking a loss of nearly $600,000. Common sense was not used when making this loan. No property was worth $1,400,000 if the purchase price was $800,000! It was one of the worst loan committee decisions I have ever seen.

—R. STUBLER—

Chapter 4

There is a Dog under my Bed!

In 1980, my family and I were camped out in Eastern Oklahoma on our annual deer hunt. My father had four brothers and they all have sons and each year we would gather together to camp and deer hunt. This particular year, twelve of us were in a tent that was big enough for eight. The tent had come from Uncle Wendell. Each member of my family has "specialties," something they are known for or something we know on them. Wendell's specialty was going to garage sales and coming up with bargains. His other specialty was not getting out of his pickup when he was hunting, but I'll not dwell on that subject because he gets kind of sensitive about it. That year, he had come up with a funeral tent, the kind they use to put over open grave sites on rainy days. As I look back on it, it seems kind of creepy, but we were glad to have it at the time. No one in the family had a lot of money and we were just happy to have a tent roof over our heads. The tent didn't leak much which was a nice bonus since it was getting down to 20 degrees at night.

I am not sure you can picture this: twelve men, ages 18 to 50, all on army cots carefully placed around the inside of the funeral tent so you could barely walk around inside. When you have twelve smelly men in a confined space, strange things can and do happen. (Didn't they do tests a few years ago on too many rats in small cage? Didn't they kill each other?) Not to say that my family is like a bunch of smelly rats, but you should be around them after a week when they have been using deer musk as a deer lure and they have not had showers.

Each member of my family has strong opinions on just about any subject. Ask any one of them about any topic and they will enlighten you. Sports? Uncle Lindsay would tell you that professional football has been fixed since the late sixties. Politics? Uncle Joe would explain that Republicans have controlled this country after Nixon secretly declared himself Emperor in 1971. Women? Cousin Derrick would tell you exactly how to handle them in any situation. Pancakes? Cousin Wayne would tell you how to eat them. It would get pretty old hearing this for a week each year for twenty years. The thing that frustrated me was that I knew the correct answers to these questions. But would my family listen to me? No. Here I was with this wealth of knowledge and they would not listen to me. You just can't talk to some people.

Bed time at a deer camp can get pretty funny. The older guys remind me of old hounds getting ready for a nap: they will circle the bed a couple of times, make a few grunts, and then settle down. The younger guys are like young hounds: they will bark about what great hunters they are, notice that no one seems to care, and then drift off to sleep.

The third night on this hunt turned out stranger than most. First, I have to explain something. I have one cousin that I will just call Cuz. His specialty is trapping and telling whoppers. He has a real knack for trapping and ran a good trap line for several years. But he can tell you some of the most outrageous stories you have ever heard. Those who know him just accept him as he is: full of bull. Those who don't, well, heaven help them. Knowing that you have to take Cuz with a grain of salt will help you understand the following, told as it occurred. We were all just settling in when Cuz began to stir in the far right corner of the tent. It was about 10:00 and it was absolutely pitch black in the funeral tent.

Cuz said, "There is something under my bed." As I stated earlier, these younger guys tend to bark like young hounds so no one really paid any attention to this.

"There is something under my bed," Cuz exclaimed. Now I am not sure why I paid attention to this comment. I think it was the tone of voice he used. It was not the typical-eighteen-year-old, I-can-whip-the-whole-lot-of-ya'll tone Cuz normally used. No, this was the I-am-glad-I-am-not-in-this-tent-alone tone. I know that tone well, having had to use it once when a bear came to visit.

"There is something under my bed," Cuz stated with a little more fervor.

"Well, what is it," asked my father, somewhat annoyed. Dad's sack time was precious to him and he didn't take kindly to interruptions.

"There is something under my bed and I think it's a dog," Cuz said. Now, I don't know if you and eleven other men have ever camped out in the woods in Eastern Oklahoma, but believe me, you don't want strange things coming in the tent with you at night. One year we had returned to camp at 10:00AM and found a huge bull in our tent so we knew animals could get into the tent uninvited. Cuz had our attention. Uncle Lindsay said, "Someone get a light." Each of us had flashlights by our beds and I was thankful to Lindsay for this good advice. I don't have a clue why we hadn't thought of this sooner. As I began to search for my flashlight, I squinted my eyes and visually searched Cuz's area of the tent, which was

only about five feet from the end of my bed. I could make out a moving shape, but because it was so dark, I could not tell what it was. Visions of coyotes or mad wolves began to creep into my mind. (My uncles and cousins won't admit it, but I think this was a common occurrence at this point.)
"There is a dog under my bed!" Cuz shouted.

I, frankly, was now concerned. Cuz's tone was shifting from I-don't-know-what-the-heck-is-happening to a I-am-getting-the-hell-out-of-here tone. I knew this tone because I had also used this tone when the bear came. We were now all searching frantically for those flashlights. Maybe it was the tension of the moment but we could not find a single flashlight!

"There's a dog in my bed and he's got a collar on," Cuz yelled. As I have indicated, Cuz is known to stretch the truth but this new information was simply impossible not to believe. If he knew it had a collar on, he must have it in his hands. I, like the others in the tent, was looking hard in that direction and could now clearly see the shape of a large dog.

Uncle Bill screamed, "My gawd, my gawd, somebody get a

light!" (Leave it to Bill to get right to the heart of the matter.) Ten flashlights pop on at once and shine on Cuz. Cuz was in his bed, looking wild-eyed, and he had hold of Uncle Joe's sock. Joe was asleep and his foot had been hitting Cuz in the side. Cuz's imagination and the darkness did the rest. We all start laughing, Cuz the loudest of all. All grown men acting like a bunch of Boy Scouts on a camp out. And Joe had slept through it all.

But I swear to you that I saw a large dog with gleaming fangs and hot steam shooting from his nose in the tent that night. How it changed into Uncle Joe's dirty sock is still a mystery.

Chapter 5

Remote Johnnys

The idea of lending money at a bank is conceptually simple: you lend money to people and businesses that will pay it back. If everyone paid you back without problem, banks would lend money to everyone. However, some people and businesses, for whatever reason, do not pay the bank back. When the borrower does not pay you back, you have to take the collateral and/or sue the borrower.

A bank tries to measure risk in a loan transaction in a number of ways. One of the methods is the Five C's of Credit, which stands for Character, Collateral, Capital, Capacity, and Conditions. Character is the borrower's reputation. Collateral is what the borrower puts up for value to back the loan; collateral can be assets like cars, equipment, or property. Capital is how much the borrower has invested in the asset or business. Capacity is a measurement of the borrower's ability to repay the loan. Conditions can be defined a number of ways, but for now, let's define it as the economic condition of the borrower. This may sound simple, but in practice it can get very interesting. One such example came to my attention in the early nineties.

I was a junior member of loan committee and the following loan was presented:

Borrower: Remote Johnnys, Inc. (RJI)
Loan Amount: $800,000
Collateral: All the equipment that the company owned

During the loan discussion, the loan officer, Bill, told the committee that RJI had been a customer of the bank for ten years, had always been profitable, and had always paid its loans on time. RJI had substantial deposits with the bank which is always a great start to getting a loan approved. The owner of the business, Johnny Sample, had excellent credit and had a strong financial statement. The cash flow of the business was more than sufficient to cover the loan payment. The loan committee reviewed the financials of RJI for about thirty minutes and you could tell the loan was about to be approved.

One of my weaknesses or strengths (depending on how you look at it) is that I always look at things a little differently than other bankers. One of my mentors many years ago told me that I should always look at a bank loan as a transaction where the bank was buying the collateral for the amount of the loan and the borrower had two options as time went along. Option one was when everything went as planned and the borrower paid the loan and kept the collateral. Option two was when things did not work as planned and the borrower "let" the bank keep the collateral.

So, as I looked at the proposed RJI loan, a question arose in my mind. Here is how the discussion proceeded.

Me: "Bill, tell me more about what RJI does."

Bill: "They provide equipment for the construction industry, like I wrote in the loan memo." (Bill was not happy to have me asking questions just as his loan was about to be approved.)

Me: "What kind of equipment does RJI provide? What will our collateral be?"

Bill, unhappier still: "We will have all the assets of the business."

Me: "Tell me what those assets are, please."

Bill: "RJI provides remote johnny's (porta potties) to construction sites."

Me: "So our collateral on this loan is primarily porta potties?"

Bill (really not happy): "Yes. But I want you to remember that this is a good business that has proven its ability to cash flow its debt."

Me: "Bill, I understand that RJI is a good customer but what would happen if he could not pay the loan? Would we even know where all these porta potties were located?"

Bill: "Well, ah, I think we would have a list of where they are located."

Me: "How many porta potties does it take to be collateral on $800,000 loan?"

Bill: (no answer).

Me: "Ok, let's say RJI does not pay us and we find all these porta potties all over Dallas and Ft. Worth. Where do we store them once we get them in our possession?"

Bill: (no answer).

Me: "Finally, let's assume we have the porta potties in our possession. Who is going to buy them from us so we can get our money back?"

From there, it was all downhill. There was no chance that RJI's loan was going to be approved. The Loan Committee, up to that point, had covered four C's of credit but did not pay enough attention to the fifth C – collateral. I had taken back enough collateral on loans at that point in my career to always be thinking about how would we get our hands on the collateral and how would we sell it. The loan was declined.

A year later, the economy bottomed out (pun intended), nearly all construction stopped, and another bank that made the loan took a giant loss. I have never forgotten the porta potty loan discussion.

As one may imagine, I was not always the most popular guy with other lenders due to my questions in loan committee.

Chapter Six

Eyes

I am not sure why we decided to start predator calling. I think we read an article in "Outdoor Life" and got excited about the idea. I was sixteen, and my best friend, Keith, was fifteen. We were anxious to try predator calling.

We had heard men talk about predator calling and now, armed with the knowledge from "Outdoor Life", we went to Walmart to purchase a call. (I have heard it said that you can get everything you need in life from Walmart.)

Walmart had three different kinds of calls: a Distressed Rabbit call (what it was distressed about was uncertain), a Hurt Fox Pup call, and a Lost Kitten call. Keith and I had a serious discussion. We had both heard a rabbit squall, but we had never seen a fox in the woods, much less heard one. The Lost Kitten call just seemed too sad to consider. No, the clear choice was the rabbit call. At least we knew what a hurt rabbit sounded like. I picked up the call and gave it a strong blow. I don't know if you have heard a rabbit squall, but the sound can be unnerving. Walmart immediately called a Code 23 in Sporting Goods. A woman dropped her Tide.

Keith and I decided to buy the call before further testing, after some encouragement from the sporting goods staff. We forked over the five dollars and twenty seven cents and proudly headed outside.

As we drove to Keith's house, we realized we had a problem. Most predator calling was done at night and there was no way our parents would allow us out after dark with guns. (A reasonable thought, if you knew us.) After some debate, we decided that we would slip out of Keith's house that night after his parents had gone to sleep. (My house was briefly considered, but Dad had this really nasty habit of showing up unanticipated at odd times. Like when I was doing something I shouldn't be doing.) Keith's parents were sound sleepers and he lived near the Muddy Boggy River in Atoka which we believed would be a great place to call.

About eleven o'clock, we slipped out of the house. It was one of those deep, dark nights. There was some fog and heavy cloud cover. We had come heavily armed; Keith with a semi-automatic .22 loaded to the gills with shells and me with my shotgun, loaded with buckshot. We were not sure what would come to the call, but we were loaded for bear.

We made our way down the streets, carrying our guns. (It is a good thing this did not happen today. Someone would see two kids carrying guns, think it was a gang war, and call the police. I can just see the SWAT teams pouring down on us. Not a pretty picture.) I have never really liked being out in the woods at night. You can't see where you are going and what is watching you. I got chased by mad cows one night while coon hunting with my uncles ... well, that is another story. The point is I don't like being in the woods in the dark. Keith wasn't fond of it either. We crossed Muddy Boggy and made it to a clearing about a half mile from the river.

We set up in a big brush pile. It was pitch black with no moon. We had walked the last four hundred yards without using our flashlights because we did not want to spook the coyotes and bobcats we knew were prowling about. Outdoor Life said you needed a spotlight to do this correctly, but we had spent all our money on the call. Besides, the game warden would consider anyone with a real light as an illegal deer spot lighter, which was an unacceptable risk. We had our two D-cell flashlights to spot the wild predators.

I had the honor of being the caller. I was the oldest and put up most of the money. I broke the silence with a hearty squall. The hair on my back stood up. I could hear my heart beating.

Keith whispered, "It sure sounds scary." We waited. Nothing but blackness. I waited five minutes and gave it another blow, this time a bit softer. It sounded just like a rabbit screaming. I almost screamed myself. Keith said he had to use the bathroom. I told him to be quiet. Blackness.

I gave it an even softer blow. The rabbit call squalled. Suddenly, we could sense movement out in front of the brush pile. Now I wished we had chanced a real spotlight.

We turned on our flashlights. Eyes! We could clearly see two yellow eyes, staring at us. I moved my flashlight to the left and saw another set of yellow eyes. Keith moved his and I quickly counted two more sets of eyes. Everywhere we shined the light were eyes! We were surrounded. What would have happened next we will never know. Suddenly, a moo came from one of the sets of eyes. The eyes belonged to cows. There were about fifteen of them at the brush pile, wondering what the noise was. We gathered up our stuff and headed home. Thus ended our predator calling.

I still have that call somewhere.

Chapter 7

Skin in the Game

In 2004, I was working in a Plano bank when I received a telephone call. A man named Sam said he wanted to borrow two million dollars and that he would like to come in and talk with me.

A lending officer is always trying to lend money. He or she is graded on how much he or she lends out each year, so I was eager to talk to Sam.

Sam came in the next day. He told me that he was going to buy a recreational vehicle dealership in North Dallas for three million dollars. I asked for details and he said he was putting down one million dollars and wanted to borrow two million.

As I have previously mentioned, I am always concerned about "skin in the game"- what a borrower has in a deal compared to what the bank has in the deal. So, having 33% equity in the deal was a great start.

Side note: if you will think about the mortgage crisis of 2008-2009, one of the main things that was occurring was the mortgage companies and banks were financing houses with little to no money down. No skin in the game.

I asked him if he had brought the financial statements and tax returns on the business he was buying. He said he had and gave them to me. I then asked for his personal financial statements and tax returns which he also had with him. I thanked him and asked him to return in a couple of days after I had had a chance to look over the information.

Over the next couple of days, I reviewed the tax returns and financials of the business. On paper, it appeared to be a good business and one that could support a loan of two million dollars. The business provided more than sufficient cash to play the debt over time.

I pulled Sam's credit; it was good. But as I looked over his financial information, I became concerned. He did not have a million dollars cash nor did he have assets that he could turn into a million dollars cash. He did not even have five hundred thousand in assets. He was simply not that strong financially.

Sam came back into the bank in a couple of days. I told him that I needed an explanation of how he was going to put down one million dollars on the purchase of this business. He explained that the seller was going to take back a note from the purchaser as the sale was completed. That was, by his explanation, his equity in the deal.

In my career, I have seen this approach many times. A borrower points out that since the transaction is three million and the bank is only lending two million, there is one million in "equity" in the deal.

But equity is equity and debt is debt. Sam was not going to have one million dollars of his money in this deal. Sure, the bank was only going to lend two million dollars, but Sam was going to have another one million dollars of debt in this transaction, not one million dollars in equity. I told him I wanted to think about this overnight and to come back in the next day. For the remainder of the day, I did some research on Google. After some time, here is what I discovered. Sam had been the broker for selling this RV dealership for over two years. It had been advertised for sale for two million and there had apparently been no takers.

What happened from here is only my guess but I think it is a good one. Sam got to thinking that he had a solution for selling this business. He went to the seller and proposed a deal. Sam would buy the business for three million dollars, the seller would take a "note" for one million dollars from Sam (which would never be paid), and they would approach a bank with a deal that appeared to have lots of equity in it. Plus, Sam would get a commission check for one hundred thousand dollars for selling the business.

When we met the next day, I told Sam that we would only be interested in lending the money if he came up with a million in cash. He left the bank without much further discussion. I found out later that another bank in town loaned Sam the money and the seller got his two million dollars cash plus a note from Sam for one million dollars. After four months, Sam apparently got tired of running the business, got the most expensive RV on the lot, and drove off.

That bank had to foreclose on the business and finally found Sam and the RV in California. I am sure they took a major loss on the loan.

That was quite a scam. The borrower had no skin in the game.

-RSTUBLER-

Chapter 8

Top Dog

It was my brother-in-law that got me hooked on beagles. In 1976, I was lucky enough to meet a gorgeous young lady named Carol who became the center of my life. One thing led to another and, eventually, I went to Arkansas to meet her family. Although her family was nice (got to be careful here), it was running rabbits with beagles that really made an impression that weekend. Carol's sister was dating a fellow named Steve. As I indicated, we later all became related, but that's not the point. Steve was kind enough to take me out on a rabbit hunt that weekend. I was never the same.

I don't know if you have ever had the rare pleasure of hearing five good beagles sing their song as they chase a rabbit. If not, I can tell you that there is no sweeter sound to a dog man. I have always had dogs even when I was small. Mostly bird dogs and crossbreed mutts. The bird dogs were my father's, but I fooled around with them quite a bit. We had pointers, Brittiany Spaniels and setters, all quail hunting dogs. The mutts were mine and were good dogs, if you believe a good dog is one that will go along with a boy on his adventures. But I never really had a dog that would do something. Steve's dogs would find a rabbit, jump it out of a thicket, and run it right around in front of you. It was and is one of the easiest ways I have found to hunt.

I had to have a beagle. Carol and I married about a year later and I quickly acquired a beagle puppy out of two of Steve's dogs. His name was Bo and he was the prettiest little guy you have ever seen. He was a small beagle and I had him in brush piles looking for rabbits within the first year. But as anyone who is married to a beagler will tell you, one beagle is never enough. I soon purchased Rocky, a handsome pup out of a high-powered, registered dog. Rocky grew very quickly into a stately, fifteen inch beagle. With a group of dogs, one dog is going to be what I call Top Dog, the dominant male. (People are the same as dogs, it just isn't always as easy to see.) Bo was older than Rocky, and so in his mind, he was Top Dog. As long as Rocky was a pup, that worked fine. But within a year, Rocky had become four inches taller and more importantly, about twice as heavy as Bo. Soon the dog fights began to turn in Rocky's favor. Bo would challenge him about once a week. It would be over a food dish or a favorite sleeping spot. I would let them go, knowing that they would work it out in their own dog ways. Rocky would wrestle Bo and finally have to hold him down by the throat to get him to quit. But Bo just would not accept Rocky as superior. After all, he reasoned he had been Top Dog before Rocky came along and he would beat him some day.

Bo kept challenging Rocky about once a week. Rocky would put him in his place but seemed to get tired doing it weekly. When Rocky was about two, he did something to make me punish him. I don't remember what it was, but I was aggravated at him. He was a sweet dog who rarely did anything to annoy me so this was unusual. I was standing over him scolding him. Rocky was holding his head down looking guilty when Bo attacked out of nowhere. Bo lit into him and looked at me as if to say, "Come on, Ken, it's you and me against him." Rocky, not expecting this sneak attack was caught off guard and Bo had a real advantage. Bo looked at me as if to say, "Let's get him!" I backed off and stayed completely out of it, much to Bo's disappointment. Bo got beat again and I think he never understood why I didn't help him beat up Rocky.

Five years later, I was down to two beagles. I had owned a number of beagles during that time, but only had Rocky and Ann, a little female, left. (After five years, I took pity on Bo and gave him to a friend of mine in my hometown. He got to be Top Dog again there.) One day, I let Rocky and Ann run a rabbit behind the house and they both got after a deer and ran so far I could not hear them. Normally, I always keep a collar on my dogs with my name and telephone number. I was upset because I had taken Rocky's collar off of him due to a rash on his neck. I looked for them all evening, but they did not come back. The next day, I got a call from a man who had found little Ann dead next to the highway. Now, I am a grown man, but I will tell you, I cried like a baby as I buried that sweet little female hound. Rocky was nowhere to be found. I placed a lost dog ad in the paper offering a reward. No response.

Ten days later, I got a call from a friend of mine who had heard a neighbor say that a beagle had come up to his place. I broke several laws driving out to the man's place which was about ten miles from my home. When I got there, a man came to the door and said yes, they had a beagle. He asked me if I could prove that the dog under the house was mine and I was not sure what to say. He told me that his family had heard a dog running something for four days and nights when this dog came limping up in their yard. He said they fed the dog, but the dog would not let anyone touch him. The man said the dog was sore from running so long that he could barely walk. I knew it had to be Rocky since he just plain loved to run anything. He said the dog was under the trailer but would not come out unless they left food out and went inside. The fellow asked me again how I was going to prove it was my dog.

I sat down and called Rocky's name, giving my usual whistle. Rocky stuck his head out from under the house and stiffly walked over to me. He came over and laid his big head on my knee and lay there looking at me. I stroked that big head, tears swelling up in my eyes. The man looked at me and said, "That's your dog." I gave him the reward and eased out of there before I broke down.

I had the pleasure of Rocky's company several years after that time. I don't know about dogs and the afterlife, but I have a feeling that when I cross over, Rocky will be there again to lay his head on my knee.

He was my Top Dog.

Chapter 9

Mistakes

My favorite banking stories are where I was right and others were wrong. Of course, in my career, there were many times when the opposite was true. But my favorite stories are the former and I am not as quick to tell the latter. I made many mistakes in my career and the following story is an example.

While I worked in Richardson, one of my jobs was working bad loans, the ones that no one else in the bank had been able to collect. We had a large portfolio of pool loans. A pool loan was where someone had purchased a pool and taken a second mortgage on their home. When the late eighties financial downturn hit, many people could not make their payments.

I have collected loans most of my career. It can be a very unpleasant job. I always try to give people every opportunity to work out a payment plan. Sometimes however, you have to foreclose and that is the way it is.

In 1989, I had to foreclose on a house on the east side of Richardson. All combined, there was debt of $200,000 on the house. The people in the house could not pay so I foreclosed on the property.

No bank wants to own property. It is always a bad deal. Potential buyers think that the bank will sell the property for a greatly reduced price and are always looking for a great bargain.

This house was one of the ugliest houses I had ever seen. It was about ten years old and had zero street appeal. It had very few windows so it was very dark inside. I talked to a real estate agent and he said I should put it up for sale for $180,000. So that is what I did, which meant I wrote off $20,000 right off the bat.

The house simply would not sell. A number of people looked at it but no one made an offer for over a year.

Finally, a man named Mark saw the house and made an offer of $160,000. Mark came into the bank and I talked with him about the house. I have to be frank and say I had a funny feeling about Mark from the moment I met him. My instinct told me not to lend to him. Something just did not seem right. But I really needed to sell this property so I ignored this instinct. This was mistake one.

He explained he had filed Chapter 13 bankruptcy six months prior when he lost his business in another state. Normally, this would have kept any bank from financing a house for him, but I really wanted rid of this house. This also meant that I was going to have to write off another $20,000 on the house.

Mark and I talked, off and on, for about a week. I explained that we would not normally finance a house for someone who had just filed bankruptcy. He said he understood but he really wanted the house. After some negotiation, I agreed to finance the house if he put down $8,000 on the purchase. He agreed to do so. My thought was that if he had $8,000 (skin in the game) in the house, he would be motivated to keep paying the bank. This was mistake two.

Closing day came around. On the day the house was closing, I received a call from the title office. There was a problem. Mark only had $3,000 to put down on the house. Mark said he still really wanted the house but he had not received some money he was expecting so all he had was $3,000. I thought about it for a while and then called the title office and said to go ahead and close the loan (after increasing the loan $5,000) so Mark could buy the house. I really wanted rid of this house. The bad thing was that after paying the title company fees, we would have virtually no money down on the loan. This was mistake three.

Mark moved into the house. In forty five days, the first payment was due. He did not make the payment. I called, no answer. I sent letters, no response. I drove to the house after work to talk with Mark. He and his family were living in the house but they would not answer the door. After one hundred days of non-payment, I sent him a foreclosure notice. No response.

On the day before the house is to be foreclosed (which is about 145 days after he bought the house), I received a Chapter 13 bankruptcy filing from Mark. I did not know then that you could file Chapter 13 as many times as you want. (Of course, this assumes that someone who has filed Chapter 13 finds a banker silly enough to lend to him again). This was mistake four, my biggest so far.

As the bankruptcy went to court, it ended up taking over thirteen months from the time Mark bought the house for the bank to foreclose and regain ownership of the house. He and his family lived in the house for thirteen months for a grand total cost to him of $3,000. I do not think he ever planned to make a payment on the house after he purchased it. The house would have rented for over $1,000 a month so I had cost the bank a loss of $10,000 in rent. Plus Mark and his family left the house in a huge mess, which the bank had to pay to have cleaned.

I ended up selling the house later for $145,000 after we re-gained possession. I do not even want to start counting up how much my handling of this cost the bank. It was embarrassing and I should have known better. If I learned anything during that time, I learned to trust my instinct.

-R. STUBLER-

Chapter 10

Tuffy

When my father, his brothers, and his sisters were growing up, they were poor and lived in Atoka, a small town in Southeastern Oklahoma. Having a family of five boys and three girls in a small house created difficulties for my grandparents. As a result, Dad and his twin brother Joe slept on the back porch, even in the winter. The porch had screens but was open to the wind and the elements. This is key to the story about Tuffy, as you will soon see.

Tuffy was a yellow bulldog that wandered up one day and adopted my father's family when my father was fifteen. Tuffy was pretty mellow for a bulldog. His purpose in life, as far as he was concerned, was to eat and then sleep in the sun. What more can a dog ask for? Lindsay and Wendell, two of my father's brothers, had other ideas. When they would catch Tuffy taking a nap, they would sneak up on him and carefully place an empty fifty gallon trash barrel over him. Tuffy's one failing was that he was a sound sleeper and he did not wake when the trash barrel covered him. After the barrel was set, the boys would take baseball bats and pound it. I can just picture Tuffy, dreaming about some female bird dog, when all the booming went off. Tuffy did not enjoy waking to the booming in total darkness. Lindsay and Wendell would hide and watch as Tuffy emerged from the drum. Tuffy would go crazy, tearing around the yard foaming at the mouth with anger.

He saw Lindsay and Wendell rolling on the ground with laughter but paid them no mind. He had to find the jerk that had put the barrel on him. This went on for about a year. Tuffy would doze off and Lindsay and Wendell would place the barrel on him, pound it with the bats, and stand back and watch. Tuffy became more enraged with each incident. Each time it happened, Tuffy would search just a little longer for the culprit.

Late one December night, my father and Joe were sleeping on the back porch when they were both awakened by a noise. Since it was a cold clear night, my grandmother had put a mountain of handmade quilts on them to keep them warm. Peering out into the moonlight, they could see a man sneaking down the alley behind their yard. Nervously they watched as the man climbed over their back fence. They wanted to run in the house, but there were too many blankets on top of them to make an escape. The prowler was sneaking up to the back door. What Dad and Joe would have done if the fellow had made it to the back door we will never know. The prowler made a fatal error, he tipped over the trash barrel.

Tuffy awoke from his sleep like a demon possessed. He made a beeline toward the prowler, jumped in the air and chomped the prowler's rear. Tuffy had finally found the jerk that had been tormenting him and he was holding on for dear life. The prowler screamed and ran for the back gate. The prowler ran yelling down the alley with Tuffy attached. Dad said you could hear the man screaming for several blocks. Tuffy returned after thirty minutes or so.

Dad said Tuffy seemed more content after that episode. Dad's brothers did not place the barrel on him again. The prowler was never seen again.

Chapter 11

Dallas Interview

I was working at a bank in Beaumont, Texas in 1985 but I was interested in moving to Dallas if I could find a position there. Dallas banking is the center of banking in this part of the country and I felt there were many opportunities to advance my career. Plus, Dallas is much closer to Atoka, Oklahoma where most of my family lives and closer to Greenwood, Arkansas where my wife's family resides.

A friend of mine in Dallas referred me to a Dallas area bank. The owner of the bank, David, called me on the phone and asked me if I would interview with them. I said sure and flew up the next day.

When we landed at the Dallas airport, there was a man holding a sign up with the name Mixon on it. I had expected someone to meet me but I did not expect a chauffeur. When I got to the limo, I did a double-take. It was a Rolls Royce limo. I had never seen a Rolls, much less a Rolls limo.

As the limo took me to the bank from the airport, I did not know what to think. Here I was, a twenty nine year old banker, being driven to a Dallas bank in a Rolls Royce limo. What kind of bank was this?

We arrived at the bank. This was a very small bank at the outer edge of Dallas. The chauffeur introduced me to David, the owner of the bank.

David and I went to an office and he began telling me about the bank. Then he asked me to tell him my background. I explained that I was the Chief Financial Officer and Chief Operations Officer at my current position. I walked him through my background in banking from teller to loan operations to lending officer to my present position. He liked my background and said he was very interested in me.

About that time, he introduced me to his son, David, Jr. Junior was on the bank board and was my age. David, Sr. told me that Junior was going to take me to lunch.

Junior introduced me to his wife, who was very pretty, and the three of us got into the limo and went to lunch. At lunch, Junior put the sales job on me of what a great opportunity this was. He said his father was "a mover and a shaker" in this part of Dallas and that there were great things ahead. We ate lunch and then Junior had to excuse himself for a minute while he went to the restroom.

I was sitting with Junior's wife, Brenda, making small talk. I could not help but notice that she had on a wedding ring with a diamond that was about two inches long, one of the biggest I have ever seen.

A minute or so went by. Brenda leaned over, placed her hand on my thigh, smiled and said "I want you to be aware that there will be hidden benefits if you take this job." I admit, I was speechless. I just looked at her, not knowing what to say. About that time, Junior made his way back to the table and

Brenda moved her hand off my thigh. We got into the limo and headed back to the bank. I sat down again with David, Sr. "Well, Ken," David said, "I have made up my mind. I am offering you the position of Cashier and Chief Financial Officer of the bank. Starting pay will be $32,000 a year and I would like for you to begin as soon as possible, today, if that is OK." I was in disbelief. This was all too strange. I told David that I was flattered but I would need to talk this over with my wife and give it some thought.

David was not happy to hear this. He explained that his whole staff of five officers, from president to the junior officers had all quit two days prior and that he needed me to make a decision right now.

"I tell you what", David added, "if you will accept right now, I will pay you a signing bonus of $5,000." For a guy like me that was making $28,000 a year, a $5,000 bonus for signing up was a huge temptation. But it was all too strange. A Rolls limo, the fact that the whole officer staff had quit, the hand on my thigh, it was too weird.

I thanked David for the offer to sign up immediately but told him I did not make these kinds of decisions this quickly. He was disappointed but said he wanted to hear back from me as soon as possible.

I had the limo driver take me to my sister's house since she lived in North Dallas and my flight home was not until late that evening.

When my sister Sandra got home from work, I told her this incredible story (leaving out the part about the hand on my thigh, I was not ready to tell that part). She asked me the bank owner's name and I told her.

Sandra's eyes lit up. "I have heard of that guy! He is in the paper all the time. There is some real estate scandal going on out that way and this guy is in the middle of it. You want nothing to do with that guy or his bank."

The next day, I called David and declined his offer to come to work. He raised the bonus offer and the salary but I passed. Two years later, David went to jail for a real estate fraud. His bank was closed and that was the end of that.

I did not tell my wife about the hand on my thigh for a while. I should have pushed Brenda's hand away immediately but I didn't do it. I was still very young and naïve at 29 and it just surprised me at the time. But I did tell my wife eventually. She just laughed.

That was quite the interview.

Chapter 12

The Slough

How can I tell you about Neal Jenkins, my best friend? No words can do him justice or punish him enough.

Neal and I met in the late eighties in Garland. He was a member of the Garland Rotary Club and I had just joined. He and I had talked a couple of times but I really did not know him very well.

I am working at the bank one day and a new customer came into the bank. Rob had just moved to town, opened a business, and was looking for a good banker. He and I talked for a bit and he told me he was interested in becoming active in the community. I told Rob that I had just joined Rotary the previous month, was going to a lunch meeting in 15 minutes, and he was welcome to come as my guest. He was flattered to be asked and agreed to be my guest.

I took Rob to the Rotary lunch and introduced him to most of the members. Rob and I sat down at a table and Neal came over and sat to my right. After we started to eat and talk a bit, I introduced Neal to Rob. Neal said hello to Rob. Then Neal put his arm around me, kissed me on the cheek and told Rob that he and I were lovers.

My mouth dropped open. Rob's did the same. Neal just

smiled. Then the program started and all talk ended.

I have nothing against gay people, but I am not gay. Neal had assumed that Rob was a longtime client of mine so he would get the joke. Rob was not, obviously, a longtime client. I drove Rob back to the bank after the meeting and tried to explain that Neal was just kidding. But Rob was not buying it. When we got back to the bank, Rob got in his car and left. I never saw Rob again, either at the bank or at Rotary.

About a year later, I took my two children, Beth and Drew, to a Rotary lunch. I lectured both of them on how they had to behave and act right. We got there and Neal spent the whole lunch shooting rubber bands at them. My kids did not know what to do. Neal just grinned the whole time.

Neal is like a brother from another mother to me. We are a lot alike.

In 2008, I found a place to lease for duck hunting in Oklahoma. It was about 125 miles from Dallas where I lived but it was a very "ducky" looking slough.

Before season, Neal and I drove up and worked on clearing it out. It was a man-made slough right next to a country road about 30 miles east of Durant, Oklahoma. It was about 100 yards wide and 300 yards long. It had been created in a low spot in a field to hold water that ran off of the big hill behind it. It had a very cool pipe drain that you could use to drain the slough.

We went up three times in the pre-season to work and clear out the place. We even hired a farmer that lived one mile down the road to do some plowing for us on the slough while it was drained. The only issue with the farmer, Keith, was that he was worried that we were going to deer hunt on this lease. Even though Keith did not hunt this property, he hunted the property that was near the slough. (Oklahoma deer hunters are always worried about someone shooting "their" buck). We reassured Keith that we were only duck hunting this property. However, 2008 turned out to be a drought year and the slough never filled up with water so we could not hunt it. Luckily, the owner of the property understood and let us have it for free the following year.

When 2009 came around, we worked the property and plant-ed some crops. Finally, the area received two weeks of solid rain just before the second part of the duck season in Oklaho-ma was to begin. Although we had not visited the slough for two weeks, I was sure that it was ready to hunt.

So, at 3:30AM on a Saturday morning, Neal, my son Drew, and I drove up to Oklahoma. We were half way there when Neal realized that he needed hip waders for the type of hunt-ing we are going to do. I knew a place that was open at that time of the morning near the Texas/Oklahoma border, so we stopped and he bought waders.

When we were about 30 minutes away, we began to discuss how we were going to hunt. "I think we should hunt the island," I said. There was a little island in the center of the slough when it was full of water. After some debate, we set-tled on this.

We reached the slough at 5:30. We put on our waders, got our hunting bags and chairs, got the decoys, let my lab, Rip, out of his box, and headed to the levy. When you approached the levy, you could not see the water in the slough until you were on top of the levy. So we walked about fifty yards before we popped up where we could see the water.

There was virtually no water in the slough. There was a tiny puddle that was about five feet wide, twenty feet long, and two inches deep and that was it. Not enough water for duck hunting. There should have been enough water to cover three football fields.

Here we were with all this hunting gear and there was virtually no water. To say we were disappointed would be a major understatement.

We laughed and talked a few minutes. Neal said, "Well, let's go somewhere and eat breakfast." Typical Neal to think of his stomach in a crisis!

"No," I said, "I got up at 3:00 and drove 125 miles to hunt a place that we have paid for. We are going to hunt." With that, I walked out and put out decoys. I had to break the ice on what little water there was to do so, but I put out the decoys.

Neal and Drew asked me, "Are you crazy? There is not enough water here to hunt!"

I told them we were staying, and after a lot of protest, Neal and Drew set up their chairs. (When I make up my mind to do something, it is difficult to stop me from doing so. Also, I had the truck keys so they had little choice in the matter). So, there we were, sitting on a tiny puddle of water in a slough that was virtually dry.

After the sun came up, no ducks came by. (No surprise). In about thirty minutes, a truck came down the road. In the position we were in, the people in the truck could see that we were sitting in the middle of a dry field.

Neal whispered, "Lord help us. Be real still and maybe they will not see us."

Neal had a great point. Here we were, the three of us, sitting out in a nearly dry field with our decoys out. A sane person would assume we were crazy.

We finally decided to leave about twenty minutes later. It was silly to keep sitting there in 30 degree weather. Just as we got to our pickup, farmer Keith drove up. We talked for a minute and he said, "Well, I drained the slough a couple of weeks ago. It was getting over into to my field and getting it wet." I just stood and stared at Keith. He had no right to go on our property. He had drained the slough just so we would be unable to hunt it. I was so mad I could not see straight. I wanted to throttle farmer Keith but better judgement prevailed. We got in the truck and drove home.

We did look pretty silly sitting in full camo by that little puddle, though.

Chapter 13

Con Men

I have always been fascinated by Con Men. Perhaps it is because I was conned out of money when I was working at my first job at a gas station when I was fourteen. A con man quick changed me and the station lost about $70. I was furious as was the station owner.

To be clear, I despise con men. They steal honest people's money, many times from those who can least afford to lose anything. A con man is the lowest form of scum.

In my career, I have seen all kinds of con men: small fraud specialists, roofing frauds, worm farm con artists (that is quite a story), and con artists who target community development. One of the best (meaning he was great at stealing from people) con men I met was in 1989 while I was working in Garland. I will call him Roy. Roy owned a car wash equipment business. Sometime in the eighties, he figured out a con game that ended up making him millions of dollars.

I discovered Roy's con game when I reviewed a loan that the Garland bank had made three years earlier. The customer, Bill, had retired from a major corporation after working there for forty-five years. Bill had a nice retirement plan and he had managed to save quite a bit of cash over his lifetime. Bill had always wanted to own his own business and that is how he met Roy in 1985.

Roy had purchased a closed car wash a year earlier. He had replaced the equipment and put the eight bay, self-service, car wash for sale for $500,000.

Interesting point here about Bill is that although he had worked for a major corporation for over forty five years, he had never owned a small business. I have found that most people who spend their whole careers at big corporations have a difficult time converting that knowledge into running a successful small business. I am not saying it is impossible but I am saying it is something I have rarely seen.

Roy met with Bill and Bill agreed to purchase the car wash for $475,000. Bill came to the Garland bank and agreed to put 20% down ($95,000) so he could get the loan. He had a great credit score of 800 and a significant personal financial statement.

In making the decision to make the loan, the bank had ordered an appraisal. An appraisal on a property is based on a number of factors: cost, comparable properties' sales prices and, on this type of property, the income that will come from the business. An appraiser will use the past financial information from the business to project the future income from the property. In this case, however, the car wash had been closed for years so the appraiser used traffic count and projected income to determine that value. Roy's company provided that information (based on their own traffic counts) which indicated that there was much more (projected) income than needed to service the debt of $380,000. The property was appraised for $475,000.

The bank approved the loan based on four primary factors: (1) Bill had an excellent credit score, (2) he had a strong financial statement, (3) he was putting 20% cash in the deal, and (4) the property appraised for $475,000 which meant the bank was financing 80% of appraised value and 80% of cost.

I got involved with Bill and this loan three years later. Bill came into the bank a few months after I was transferred to Garland and I became president of the bank. Bill sat down with me and told me his dilemma. He explained that the car wash was not bringing in enough money to pay half of the payment on what was now a $345,000 loan. He had been withdrawing cash from his savings for three years in order to pay the bank. He said he did not want to default on the loan, but that he had exhausted his savings and that he did not see any other alternative. We talked for two hours and at the conclusion of our discussion, he said to foreclose on the car wash and do what the bank had to do. He was a good man and he was ashamed to be in the situation he was in.

We foreclosed on the car wash. It took me time to piece together what had happened, but I did figure it out eventually.

Roy's staff greatly inflated the income that the car wash would produce. Neither Bill nor the bank nor the appraiser had any expertise in car washes so no one questioned the income information. Later, I figured out that Roy had under $200,000 invested in the car wash when he sold it so he made a profit of $275,000 on the sale.

In Bill's case, he purchased a car wash for $475,000 that should have sold for a price closer to $225,000 (based on the actual income figures we had after he owned it three years). Bill was a good man who was fleeced by an excellent con man.

If the cash flow projections had been based on real numbers, it would have been clear that the car wash could not provide the income to pay a loan of $380,000. The appraisal, based on real numbers, would have been closer to $225,000 rather than $475,000. Roy had figured out how to "game" the banking system.

Roy discovered that he could con the buyer and the bank if there were five key things in place when a buyer was purchasing a business from him. The keys were that (1) the purchaser had to have good credit, (2) the buyer had to have at least 20% cash to put down on the purchase, (3) the business had to have no current verifiable income figures, (4) the purchaser must have no experience in the particular business he is purchasing and most importantly, (5) Roy's staff had to inflate the projected income to a number that would cover the payment at least 1.25 times.

The most amazing thing about this story is that Roy continued to con people in this manner for the next thirty years. In each case, it appears his company would use the same inflated projected income approach as well as the other keys mentioned above. He and his company would get sued on occasion when the businesses failed, but he continued to play his con game. You may wonder what finally stopped him after all those years? He died.

I would not wish death on anyone. Roy took people's dreams of owning their own business and turned them into nightmares. He cheated many fine people and cost banks in North Texas millions of dollars in losses. He will not be missed by me.

Chapter 14

West Texas Goose Hunt

In 1997, I started taking clients to West Texas to hunt geese. During that time, there were over a million geese wintering in that area and the hunting could be fantastic.

Each year, I would take a group of hunters out to an area near Knox City in West Texas. There were a couple of different goose hunting outfitters there and we hunted with all of them over the next twelve years.

Goose hunters and duck hunters are different than other hunters. Some say we are a little crazy but we are probably crazier than they say. Who else would get up at 4:00AM to go out in waders and stand in water in 30 degree weather?

One year, I had seven hunters on the trip including me. Part of the group was Mark, who was CEO of his company. Mark had brought two of the officers of his company on the trip and they all loved to hunt. Mark had been a major client of mine for many years and was also my good friend.

Mark had brought his lab, Gus. The hunting lodge we were using had a rule about dogs which required the hunters to either leave the dogs in their outfitter kennel or to leave their dogs in the hunter's truck at night. The lodge did not want the dogs in the bunkhouse. Mark grumbled about this for a few minutes since his dog slept in his home at night but Mark agreed to put Gus in the kennel at bedtime.

My best friend, Neal, was on this trip with us as he usually accompanied me on each of these trips. He loves to goose hunt and he was, in effect, co-host with me since he always helped with any need my clients had. He and I had been on a number of these trips and he was always great to have along.

On most of these trips, I would go to bed before the rest of the clients. I am not much for staying up late before a hunt. Neal was the same and usually in his bunk about the same time.

This trip, I was on the bottom bunk and Neal was on the top bunk. During the night, I started to smell this awful odor. It smelled like three day old limburger cheese crossed with wet skunk. I tried to ignore it but it would slap my nose like a right cross when I tried to sleep. There was a window heater right by our bunks so I guessed that a rat must have got caught in it during the night and died. That was the only explanation I could come up with as I struggled to sleep.

What I did not know was that Mark had been the last to go to bed that night. He had taken Gus out of the kennel, walked him, and then brought him into the bunkhouse. The bunkhouse was split into two sections with four beds on one side and four beds on the other side. Mark and his group were on the left and Neal, Bruce, Drew, and I were on the right. After Mark went to bed, Gus had to potty one more time. So, like a dog will do, he did not want to potty where he was sleeping so he came over to our side of the bunkhouse. There he left a major poop just at the foot of the bunk that Neal and I were in.

Although I did not know it, Neal had struggled through the night as well. He later said the smell was so bad that his eyes were tearing up. He too could not figure out what the smell was. Finally, just before 4:00AM, he could take the odor no longer. He jumped out of bed to go to the restroom. He leaped out of the top bunk right into the dog poop.

Neal said, Well, crap!" which was appropriate for the situation. Mark came over, saw what happened, and explained that he was worried about his dog so he bought him inside. I believe that he planned to do so from the very beginning (Mark was not one to follow rules). Neal was gracious and did not shoot Mark on the spot. Mark said he had been feeding Gus jerky all that day and it must have upset the dog's stomach.

Neal and I still talk all these years later on how bad that smell was.

Neal, the clients, and I loaded up in the trucks and headed out. This trip we were hunting on a playa lake, a very shallow lake that waterfowl love. We were in a sit-down, cornstalk blind. There was my group of seven on the left and six hunters from another group on the right in the very large blind. The six other hunters on the right were from a medical company in Dallas. A couple of them were physicians and the others were officers in the company.

The head guide, Justin, told us that he would call the shots as the geese came in. This meant that he would direct our shooting so that we would maximize our effectiveness. He said he would call "Left Side" when he wanted my group to shoot and "Right Side" when he wanted the medical company group to shoot.

My group consisted of Mark and his two officers, Neal, Bruce Klingman, and my son, Drew. I knew that Mark, Bruce, and Drew were very good shooters. Although I would never say it to him, Neal was, at best, an average shooter. He had this habit of claiming any bird I shot. As a group, we were much better than average shooters.

Thirty minutes before sunup, the geese began to come in. One of the most amazing sounds I have ever heard is a flight of 50,000 geese as they float down out of the early morning sky to a playa lake. You can hear their wings flapping as they sail down, their calls filling the air. It looks like a tornado, a tornado of geese headed for the water.

When the first flight of geese came in front of us, our guide Justin called out "Left Side". My group fired eight shots and six geese fell to the ground. A few moments later, Justin called out "Right Side" and the other group fired away. Eight shots, not a single goose fell.

Justin called out "Left Side!" My group fired and seven geese hit the ground. Gun smoke filled the early morning air. "Right Side," he shouted a few minutes later. Shotguns roared. Not a feather was touched.

"Left Side!" Shotguns fired. Dead geese hit the ground. This continued for two hours. The medical group on the right could not hit the side of a barn with their shotguns. They shot for two hours and killed only two geese.

Because our legal limits were figured together and because each man was allowed to harvest five birds, the combined groups limit was sixty five geese. My seven hunters killed sixty three geese that morning. It was one of the finest mornings I have ever had goose hunting.

My group took pictures with the harvested geese. After we finished, the medical group took their pictures with all the harvested birds as well. I am sure that they brag about what great hunters they are to anyone who sees their pictures.

Neal thought he killed seven geese that morning. I did not have the heart to tell him how many he really killed after what he had been through getting out of bed that morning.

Chapter 15

Too Good to be True

In 2002, I had the opportunity to begin a banking relationship with a new client. Natalie was a famous athlete who had retired from her career.

As the years went by, I developed a friendship with Natalie. She maintained some of her accounts with my bank. One day, I asked her if she would put some more money with us. I told her that we had a very good rate on a CD at 5.25%. Natalie said no and added that she had just got a CD through her financial planner that paid her 8% for three years.

This made no sense to me. My bank's rate of 5.25% was one

of the highest rates in Dallas at that time and it did not seem possible that any bank in the country would be paying 8% on a three year CD. It was too good to be true.

I told Natalie that it did not seem possible that she had a CD paying 8%. She insisted that she did. She said she had known John, her financial advisor for many years and that he only handled professional athletes. I asked her if she would bring me a copy of the CD and she agreed to do so.

When Natalie came back into the bank in a couple of weeks, she told me that she still did not have a copy of the CD. I told her again that it did not seem reasonable that she had a CD that paid that rate. She picked up her phone and called her financial advisor John and asked him about her $1 million CD investment. Natalie and I were in my office and I could hear both parts of the discussion.

Natalie asked John if the investment she had was a bank CD. John answered yes, it was. Natalie asked if the rate was 8% for three years and John said it was.

She finished the call and asked me if I was satisfied. (At this point, I must point out to you that Bernie Madoff and Allen Stanford financial Ponzi scam stories had not broken so most people were not as quick to suspect financial advisors).

I told her that it did not make sense that John had found a bank that would pay 8% on a CD. I said that I could be wrong, but that I thought something was fishy. I asked her not to tell John that I thought there might be fraud involved but also advised her that I knew a CPA firm in Dallas that handled some local athletes. I asked her to get that CPA firm involved in her investment. This $1 million represented the majority of Natalie's net worth, so I was concerned.

The next day, she sent a number of emails to John. In one of her emails, she said that I told her that John was defrauding her and copied me on the email! I was disgusted at Natalie at this point since I had asked her not to bring up my name. John sent me a very hot email, telling me to mind my own business.

In two weeks, Natalie returned to the bank. She had brought a copy of her "CD," which turned out not to be a CD at all. She said that John had invested her $1 million in a business loan from Compass Bank. She had a copy of a $30 million loan that Compass had made to a company and explained that John had invested in this loan on her behalf.

This was so wrong on so many levels. John had told Natalie on the phone that she had a CD (which was untrue). He had then told her that he had invested in a bank loan but she had a copy of the original loan and no proof that she had an "investment" in that loan. Most importantly, banks do not sell part of a business loan to individuals as investments.

That finally got her attention. She spent the next twelve months trying to get her money out of this "CD." John finally paid her the $1 million she had invested with him. About twenty four months later, John's "investments" were exposed as a Ponzi scheme and his clients lost over $8 million dollars. Natalie managed to keep all of her savings.

If something appears too good to be true, perhaps it is not what it seems to be.

Chapter 16

Tracking Job

When I was growing up, my family and I deer hunted on Ten Mile Creek in Southeastern Oklahoma. Ten Mile is a beautiful place; clear running streams and miles and miles of rough, rocky mountains. Ten Mile is not an "official" mountain, the hills are all too low to meet the standards for actual mountains. However, if you ever hiked up one of those hills, you would call it a mountain too.

One thing I treasured about Ten Mile was that you could hunt all day and not see another human being. It seemed as if you were the only one out there and the year was 1874, not 1974. There were never great numbers of deer on Ten Mile. We hunted there because it was one of the few places you could hunt without paying to hunt. Deer season in Oklahoma lasted only ten days at that time. Many years the majority of us hunted the whole season on Ten Mile without seeing a buck. Some years, we would get excited over seeing a fresh deer track.

One of the most appealing features of Ten Mile was that, every ten years or so, someone would kill a monster buck. Ten Mile produced some really fine deer, heavy horned bucks that any hunter would be proud to hang on his wall every now and again. This helped a hunter stay on his stand when he had not seen a single deer all week.

In 1974 during my first year in college, I invited my friend, Keith, to go to deer camp with us. Normally, our deer camp was primarily a family affair: my father and his four brothers as well as a good number of my male cousins. There were also some friends of the family that hunted with us, depending on the year. We would have between five and fifteen male members of the family together each year. (Females were never invited. This was the seventies before we began to question this sort of thing. Today, we would probably be in court on this matter.) Keith was a senior in high school and delighted to be invited.

Opening morning, we awoke to five inches of snow on the ground. Thirty minutes before daybreak, Keith and I headed down a trail to a place where I had seen a deer the year before. (Having seen a deer in this area a year prior classified this as a "Secret Spot" in our deer camp. Secret Spots were a valuable commodity on Ten Mile and I have seen my relatives do some interesting things to obtain the location of someone's Secret Spot. In fact, Uncle Joe had been known to trail someone for miles in order to discover their Secret Spot.)

I took Keith to a clearing 200 yards down the creek past my Secret Spot and I walked back to settle in for daybreak. (I wasn't about to put my buddy in my best spot even though he was a guest. There are some things you just don't do!) Keith and I had agreed that we would stay in our stands at least two hours before getting up and meeting each other.

I had been on my stand about 45 minutes when I saw Keith, walking toward me about 150 yards down the creek. He was walking along, whistling with his .30-30 over his shoulder. I was not happy. Here it was 45 minutes into opening morning, the best time to see a buck, and he was already walking back to my area.

I lost sight of Keith as he continued to walk toward me. Suddenly, he shot. Once, twice, three times, followed by three more quick shots. There was a beaver dam down near where I had seen him and I just knew that Keith had shot the beaver. I was worried that my father and my uncles would be furious over unnecessary shooting on opening morning. Unnecessary shooting on opening morning was too terrible a sin for me to consider. I hurried down to Keith's location.

"What the heck are you shooting at," I demanded. Keith said he was walking up the creek when a huge buck broke out of the brush across the creek and began to run across an opening about thirty yards from him. (Toward me, I will always remember.) Keith's .30-30 rifle held six shells and he shot three of them as the buck went from right to left across the opening. Then, the buck turned and ran back across the opening again, left to right, and Keith fired his last three shells. (Now, I ask you, how many deer will turn and run back by so you can shoot at them again, like some shooting gallery? It has never happened to me.)

Keith and I sprinted across the creek. There on the ground in the snow was a solid blood trail that went off into the woods. I told Keith that the buck was obviously hit hard and that we should sit still for forty five minutes before we began to track the buck. Keith agreed. But the blood trail was so bright red in the white snow and we were excited so we waited all of five minutes before we started following the blood trail.

Trailing a shot deer is usually difficult work; I had done it with father and my uncles on dry ground when it took an hour to trail a buck one hundred yards. This was more like driving down a highway. There was blood on the snow about every six inches and we simply had to follow the path. The buck's trail headed uphill. About 100 yards up the hill, we found a place where the buck had laid down for a few minutes before moving on. I told Keith we needed to stop and let the buck lay down again so he would die. Keith agreed.

As we waited, it was as if the bright red blood trail was asking us to come and follow. It was a huge temptation to continue to follow the path. I knew we should wait but we could not. We trailed the buck on up the hill. We found two more places where the buck tried to lay down and die. I am sure the buck heard and smelled us as we came up the hill so he continued to get up and move on.

But we kept following. Never saw him, but we knew we were close. Finally, at the top of the hill about four hundred yards from where we started, we found a place where the buck had stopped. There was a six foot round blood spot on the snow where the buck had rested. I absolutely knew that we had to stop and let the buck lie down and die. I made Keith sit with me and we waited thirty minutes.

This next part is difficult for me to tell. When we got up, we could not find where the buck left this spot. The six foot spot was there but there was no blood trail or tracks leading from it. We could not believe it. It was as if the deer had flown off the earth in a helicopter. We nervously began making larger and larger circles around the spot. Nothing. We repeated the effort. Still nothing. I was speechless. All I knew to do is what I usually did when I had trouble: go get Dad. We marched to camp like a defeated army.

One by one, my uncles and cousins came back to camp. We told the story anew to each family member. The sun came out and the day began to warm up. By the time my father came into camp two hours later, it was fifty degrees and virtually all the snow had melted. Uncle Bill, Uncle Lindsay, Dad, two of my cousins, Keith, and I walked back to where Keith had shot the buck.

Keith and I indicated, as best we could, where the blood trail had been and my family began to search for signs. Keith and

I were discouraged because the snow was gone and with it, the blood trail that had been so easy to see. Slowly, Dad and my uncles picked up the trail. I don't know how they did it, but they did. Uncle Lindsay was the best tracker in the family with my father a close second. My cousins helped as we crept along, following the signs. I could not tell for sure what my father and uncles were seeing, but slowly and surely they figured out where the buck had gone.

For hours we worked out the trail. Lindsay would study the ground and Bill and my father would ease ahead and look for tracks or blood. Slowly and surely, we moved along. Finally, after two hours of tracking, we found the buck, dead on the side of a hill. Dad explained that the buck doubled back on us for about 50 yards which caused Keith and me to originally lose the trail.

The buck ended up being one of the best ever taken off of Ten Mile. He was a heavy deer with dark thick horns, a ten pointer, with a nineteen inch spread. Keith had first timer's luck and did not realize it. He was only 17 and did not know that killing a great buck like that on opening morning might never happen to him again, ever.

The ability to track a wounded deer through the woods is a skill. Uncle Lindsay, Uncle Bill, and my father tracked the wounded buck 500 yards after the snow had melted. It was truly amazing. Those three were far better woodsmen than I will ever be.

Chapter 17

Know your Collateral

I was working at a bank in Garland in January, 1989. This was the first time I was a bank president and I was determined to do as good a job as possible.

The bank had a customer named James who owned an auto parts store. James had owned the business for over twenty years and had been a customer of the bank the whole time.

After I had been at the bank a couple of months, James came in to see me. James and the previous bank president had had a close relationship for a very long time. James was anxious about whether he would get the same treatment from me that he had received from the previous president.

He told me that his business needed to borrow $25,000 from the bank for working expenses and inventory. I pulled his loan file and saw that there was little financial analysis in the file. The previous bank president had done business with people based on the character of the borrower. In James's case, he had known him twenty years and James had always had a good reputation with the bank. He already had a loan to the bank with a balance of almost $200,000 secured by the inventory of the auto parts business. His business leased space in a building so that was not available for collateral.

I asked James for current financial statements. He was not happy to be asked this question. He told me of his relationship with the previous president and how long he had banked with my bank. "Why would you need current financial statements?" he asked. "I have always been able to walk in here and get what I ask for!"

I told him that I was sorry and that I would love to do what he was asking me but that I could not do so without current financial information. James reluctantly agreed to bring in the information.

The next week, he bought in the information. In those days, we analyzed a company's financial statements by hand so I begin to spread his financial statements. I worked for about an hour and then sat looking over the summary of the last four years. Something was bothering me about the financials but I could not put my finger on it at first.

Finally, it dawned on me. For the four years I was reviewing, his inventory totals never changed. It never changed by one cent. For years ending 1985, 1986, 1987, 1988, the dollar figure listed for inventory cost was exactly the same - $245,137.33. With any business, the inventory totals will increase and decrease as the business sells and buys its goods. There was no possible way that the inventory would be exactly the same amount, year after year. There was something rotten with his financial statements. The bad news was that the bank's collateral was inventory.

I hired a firm to do an inventory review. It turned out that there was only about $100,000 in inventory in the whole store. James had been selling inventory and ignoring his financial records for years (and not paying the bank down on his line of credit). He was just "plugging" a number for inventory on his financial statements. The bank had gotten too comfortable with its borrower and had been negligent in reviewing the financial statements. The bank did not require inventory listings on a regular basis and never did a "real" review of the borrower's collateral.

James was obviously dishonest but he was led to ruin by a banker who did not do his job. The banker did not know what his collateral was or what it was worth. In the end, the bank took more than a $150,000 loss due to not monitoring its collateral. James ended up losing his business.

What a mess!

-R. STUBLER-

Chapter 18

Up a Tree

When I was fifteen, my sister married Dan, a bow hunter. Dan was my introduction to bow hunting. I had been deer hunting with guns since I was twelve and was ready to do anything that gave me a chance to kill a deer. (Come to think of it, I haven't changed that much in fifty years!)

So I purchased (with Dad's money) a fine Fred Bear recurve bow. For those of you not familiar with archery, this was a natural bow; no pulleys or sights or magic releases. You just pulled it back and let it fly. I practiced with it and got where I could consistently hit a pie pan from thirty yards. I figured I was ready.

Bow season arrived. Dan seemed excited to have me go with him. (At least he appeared that way in front of my sister.) Opening morning, we headed out long before daybreak. We walked four hundred yards off a dirt road and entered a big field. Imagine a football field, but it is two hundred yards long with a huge oak in one end zone.

So, Dan said to me, "Ken, you climb up the tree. It will be a good place to see a buck." Then he left.

Now, I was no expert on deer back then, but I had been hunting enough with my father to know that this setup might not be the best I had ever seen. First of all, there were no deer trails nor was there any deer sign in the field. Deer sign in the place you are hunting is always a good thing.

Speaking of deer sign, Dan had pulled a good one on us the previous year. My cousin John, Dan, and I were walking along and saw some deer droppings. As we looked at them, John wondered out loud if they were fresh. Dan reached down, picked one up, and popped it in his mouth. "About four hours old," he said. We were stunned by this action. Later we discovered that Dan had palmed a Milk Dud in his hand when he reached down and he put that in his mouth rather than the dropping. So I knew a few things about deer sign and about Dan.

I climbed the tree. There was not a good limb to sit on so I was standing on a limb next to the trunk about twenty feet in the air. I do not know if you have ever stood on a tree limb for about thirty minutes and watched the sun come up. I am here to tell you that you do not care how pretty it is because it is damn uncomfortable to stand on a tree limb that long.

Another thirty minutes passed. There had not been a sign of a deer or a squirrel, or a rabbit, or even a bird for that matter. Did I mention it is tough to stand in a tree?! I began to think about Dan's attitude before he left. Was it me or did he seem relieved to have a place to stick me? Did he seem happier when he left? What kind of guy was he?

(Nothing was happening in the field.)

Say, was he laughing as he left, I wondered?

One of the bad things about bow season, you cannot hear if anyone else is getting a shot.

I said to myself, "Man, he did seem eager to drop me off. I think I have been had."

There is just no way to be comfortable while standing in a tree. After an hour, I had had enough. I got my rope out of the bag and tied it on the bow so I could lower it down from the tree.

Just then, I heard something. It was far away in the distance but it definitely sounded like "something."

My rope was thirty feet long and it was attached to my bow with the remainder hanging down the trunk of the tree.

The sound was getting louder. It sounded like a horse running.

I looked down to the end of the field. I could not see anything in the field but I could tell that the sound was coming from the woods at the other end of the field.

Suddenly, out came a big buck. He was galloping just like a racehorse and was headed right for me.

I wondered if I should get the rope off my bow. But there was no time! He was coming right at me.

I watched him come. I thought, "Man, that looks like a good deer. Won't everyone be surprised when I bring him in. I will be the Best Hunter in the family."

On he came. One hundred fifty yards away.

My breathing increased. My heart started to pound.

One hundred yards away now.

My breathing was much louder now. I shut my mouth so I would not make so much noise.

On he came. Fifty yards away from me now, headed right for me.

Shutting my mouth was not helping. I was really breathing hard now and my nose was simply not equipped to handle the volume. I was blowing like a train whistle and my heart was thumping like a runaway train.

Forty-five yards now.

I decided I had to do something to stop the noise from my nose. (You have to be quiet to kill a big buck!) So I placed my hand over my nose and my mouth and tried to completely muffle the whole group. Big mistake. This only made it worse. Much worse.

Picture this: I was up a tree with a rope hanging down from my bow. I was wheezing through my nose and mouth with my hand trying to stop the airflow (much like a monkey drunk on fermented fruit).

The buck stopped at thirty yards and looked up at me in the tree. He stood perfectly still for one minute, just staring at me in the tree. He had, apparently, never seen a drunken monkey wheezing and blowing air up in a tree before and the sight confused him. Then he snorted and slowly circled the tree, staying about thirty yards from the tree but never taking his eyes off me until he completed the half circle and moved on. Meanwhile, I continued to wheeze, cough and snort as I tried to breathe. I never came close to shooting.

Later when Dan came back, he asked me why I did not shoot. With one hand on my nose and mouth and the other hand holding me in the tree, I ran out of hands. I had the worst case of deer fever I have ever seen.

Chapter 19

Loan Approvals

In the late eighties, I was working for a bank in Dallas owned by a large bank holding company when we were purchased by another bank group. At this time, each bank had its own charter. This meant that each bank had a President, Cashier and a Board of Directors. The bank was owned by a holding company and had to answer to the holding company but it had some degree of independence, at least in theory.

After the new group purchased the bank and sixty days had passed, we received a loan package from the holding company. It was a loan request for $10 million, part of a $125 million loan. Due to the way each bank in the holding company had separate charters, it was going to have to be "participated" among the banks. In other words, our bank would have to approve $10 million and the rest of the bigger banks in our holding company group would each take their share of the remaining $115 million, depending on how much they could take on with their legal lending limits. (Today, bank holding companies like Wells Fargo and Bank of America have one charter, with the offices being branches which means none of this participating goes on in the huge banks).

The president of the bank, Dan, gave me the loan package. He told me to review the package and come back with a recommendation.

The loan package was huge, two hundred pages. It was not an easy package to analyze. Just the description of the collateral was fifty pages.

The purpose of the loan was to pay off another loan of approximately the same amount. Some of the very interesting features of the loan were that the borrower (who I will call the RC family) was in Spain and the collateral (real estate and other holdings) was all in Spain. This was extremely unusual for a Texas banking group to be considering a loan to Spanish clients with Spanish collateral. The head of the new bank holding company wanted the bank to do international business and this was to be the first of this kind of business for the bank.

The collateral on the loan was valued at $175 million. However, the bank was accepting the value of the collateral based on information from the borrower. I had never seen that before. (Never a good idea).

I worked on the package for a couple of hours and finally decided to look at the request in a simple manner. The loan request was $125 million and the rate on the loan was 10%. That meant that the RC family needed to have $12.5 million in cash flow (income) to pay just the interest on the loan each year. As I reviewed the financials of the family, I was surprised to see that the family had nowhere near the cash flow to pay the interest each year. In fact, they did not have half of that amount to pay the interest.

After some thought, I wrote up a one page memo that summarized my findings. In my opinion, we should not approve the loan. Further, if we did approve the loan and it closed, it would be a "classified" loan (bad loan) the day it funded. I presented my memo to the president. He spent some time looking at my memo and the loan package and then called me back to his office.

Dan: "Send a fax to the holding company office and tell them we are passing on this loan request and tell them why."

So I did as he requested and did not think much more about it for the next hour. At the end of the hour, I got a fax back from the main office. Here is what it said:

Dan and Ken:
By the end of today, one of two things is going to happen. Option one is that the two of you are going to approve the loan. Option two is that the two of you are not going to approve the loan, we are going to fire you both, hire your replacements, and your replacements are going to approve this loan.

Sincerely,

Holding Company Senior Management

That was as clear of an instruction as I have ever received in my career. We approved the loan. In truth, we had a fiduciary responsibility to disapprove the loan. We were doing a disservice to our shareholders at the bank. But we had no choice and we approved the loan.

After the loan was closed and funded, the RC family never made a single payment on the loan. The bank group started foreclosure procedures and then discovered that it takes years to foreclose on property in Spain. In addition, the RC family was very connected in Spain and was apparently able to put political pressure on Spanish judges and courts, so this took forever. I am sad to say that this group of banks I was working for failed in the coming years and this loan was a major factor in the failure.

I have a rule about working for a company. When a company asks you to do something, you should do it as long as it is not illegal or immoral. You may not like what you are being asked to do but you need to do it. This loan approval was not illegal, but it came very close to immoral.

It was a loan that I will never forget. Any borrower who never makes a single payment tends to stick in my mind.

Chapter 20

The Great Goose Hunt

In the fall of 1976, I was just starting my junior year at Oklahoma Baptist University. My cousin John was a freshman and my roommate.

During that time, the State Fish and Game Department was allowing public goose hunts at the Tishomingo Refuge. In those days, 300,000 geese wintered at Tishomingo (or Tish as we locals called it). I had visited Tish a number of times while I was growing up since it was only 35 miles from my hometown of Atoka. At Tish, you could get within 100 yards of the geese while they were feeding without bothering them. Of course, the geese knew by experience that you could not shoot at them on that part of the refuge.

One Friday night in October, we drove down from Shawnee so we could hunt the refuge. We had no money so we did not get a hotel. I was 20 and John was 18 and we slept in the back of his pickup in sleeping bags. We parked within 200 yards of where the birds were in a field on the refuge, opened up his pickup camper shell, and settled into our sleeping bags. All night long, you could hear these 300,000 geese as they moved about the field. John and I got very little sleep as we dreamed of limiting out on geese the next morning.

At 4:00AM, we were two bleary eyed young hunters who

showed up at the check station. We were not sure what to expect. John & I had duck hunted every season since I was 16 but had never been on a goose hunt. There were about 100 hunters there at the check station so it was pretty intimidating at first.

The game rangers assigned each group of two to four hunters to a specific blind in a field. The field was about the size of a football field and there were three blinds side-to-side. Imagine three blinds across the ten yard line spread out sideline to sideline, then three blinds on the twenty, three on the thirty and so on.

Each blind was an underground bunker. You walked down a ladder into it and then you were below ground level. There was a movable top that covered the blind so the geese could not see you. It was a pretty cool setup.

John and I were in the bunker and we were fired up. We had spent seven mostly sleepless hours listening to 300,000 geese so we knew the geese were nearby. We were located in a bunker that was the equivalent of the 40 yard line so we were sure we would get our limit. John had this long barreled bolt action 12 gauge and he felt he could kill geese out to 75 yards.

Sun up finally arrived. The geese moved off a field that was three hundred yards to our south. The geese flew straight toward our field until they were one hundred yards away from our field. At that point, they flew straight up. When they reached an altitude of one hundred yards, they turned and flew over our field. It was a spectacular sight.

The maximum effective range of a twelve gauge shotgun is about 60 yards. Since these geese were one hundred yards high, they were almost impossible to hit. That, however, did not stop the hunters on this field. As the geese crossed the ten yard line, all three hunting groups on the ten yard line fired. The geese flew higher. When the geese crossed the twenty, the twenty yard hunters' group fired. The geese flew higher. By the time the geese were over John and me, they were two hundred yards high. John & I did not fire. However, some of the hunters continued to fire on the fifty and sixty yard lines.

The fly-over by the main geese group lasted forty five minutes. It was difficult to be sure, but I would say there were at least 500 shots fired at the geese during that time. One goose was killed in that time. I have no idea how he died. He probably died of old age. I do not see how any hunter could have reached him with a shotgun. No other goose was killed during this barrage of shooting.

These geese lived at the refuge. They knew exactly where the hunting field was so they knew they had to get over one hundred yards high to avoid death over this field. Once they had finished flying over our field, they dropped down to fifty yards high and continued on the wheat field that was their destination.

We were required to stay in our bunker for two hours for this hunt. Three geese were killed during the last hour and a half. These geese were unfortunate enough to fly low enough to be shot. They were probably new birds that had recently flown into the area. They were not a part of the main group that flew over that morning, so they did not know the rules. One hundred hunters killed four geese in two hours. John & I never fired a single shell. We did laugh all morning as hunters blasted away at geese over 150 yards high.

Thus ended the Great Goose Hunt of 1976.

Chapter 21

Collections

I have been making and collecting loans most of my career. You can learn a lot about life while collecting loans.

Back in 1990, the economy in Dallas had a major downturn. Construction nearly came to a complete stop and banks stopped lending on nearly everything.

I had inherited a client named Bob who was in the construction business. He had been a customer of the bank for many years and was a good man. But when the construction business dried up, he was in a bind. He owed the bank just over $1 million and he did not have the money or income to pay the loan.

The good thing for the bank was that Bob had pledged equipment as collateral for this loan that had a book value of over $1.7 million. The problem was Bob did not want to sell the equipment to pay the bank off. With construction off, it was a horrible time to sell his equipment.

Bob would not talk to me for several months. He was past due on his loan for over ninety days and it was a serious matter for the bank. But he would not talk to me. Part of me understood. If he talked to me, it would mean he would have to face his situation and he did not want to do that.

At this point, I could have started the process of forcing him to turn over his equipment to me. That would have probably turned Bob into fighting the bank and I did not want to do that if I could avoid it.

I wrote Bob a certified letter that explained the bank's position. I told him that I would rather work with him than against him. He got the message and called me. We talked several times over a ten day period and he finally agreed that he had to sell the equipment and pay his loan. There was little else he could do. He requested that he use an auctioneer that he knew and that he would hold the auction in ninety days. I agreed to this.

When the auction was sixty days away, I started to think about the process of the auction. The auctioneer would sell the equipment, the buyers would write checks for the equipment, the auctioneer would deposit those checks and finally, the auctioneer would write the bank a check for our payoff on Bob's loan. (There were some other legal details about UCC filings and releases but I will not go into that here).

Since Bob had chosen his auctioneer, the bank had little control over the auction. I had the auctioneer's name, Dave, so I called him and asked him for references. He gave me the name of his bank in Little Rock, Arkansas and the name of his banker. I explained to Dave my concerns about getting our $1 million from this auction. He told me that his banker would guarantee payment of these funds.

I called Dave's banker in Little Rock. The banker was the president of the bank and told me that Dave was a twenty year customer and the bank would honor (pay) any check that Dave wrote. I asked the president if he would put that in writing to me and he surprised me by saying that he would. In four days, I had said letter in hand.

The day of the auction I sent Cal, a young banker that worked for me to the auction. I wanted to be sure that things went as planned. Cal arrived at the auction at noon just as the sale began. During the next four hours, Cal called me and informed me that the auction was going ok. The equipment was selling. It was not bringing in as much as Dave and Bob wanted, but it was selling.

About 4:00, I got a call from Cal. He said the auction was almost over and Dave and Bob had talked to him and told him that, "since the auction was not bringing in as much as they expected, they were not going to pay me the full $1 million and wanted the bank to take $750,000 and settle for that amount." The auction was going to bring in "only" $1,200,000 and Bob wanted at least something for himself from the sale (approximately $450,000, less costs). During this period of time, there were many banks that were settling loans for less than the amount of the payoff.

I asked Cal to put Bob on the phone. Bob refused to talk to me. Dave also would not talk with me.

I told Cal to tell Dave and Bob that they had two options. Option one was that Dave was going to write the bank a check for $1 million. Option two was that they were not going to pay us $1 million and I was going to call the sheriff and have him go out and arrest them for fraud. (The truth was the sheriff probably would not have done this but I had to say something).

After some debate between Dave and Bob, they agreed to write a check for $1 million. But Dave, the auctioneer, attempted to get a little cute with me on this. He wrote the $1 million check but made it out to Bob rather than to the bank. Bob refused to endorse the check and they thought this would give the bank a problem. Bob and Dave assumed that my bank could not negotiate the check. What they did not know was that this made me mad.

Cal brought the check back to the bank and walked into my office at 6:00PM. I have an operations background and know quite a bit about endorsements. I stamped the back of the check with a stamp that said, "Pay to the order of the named payee, endorsement guaranteed by the receiving bank." As long as my bank credited the named payee (Bob), the bank in Arkansas could not question the endorsement.

Then I drove to Love Field, hopped a plane and flew to Little Rock.

At 9:00 the next morning, I was in Little Rock, Arkansas at the bank of the auctioneer. I walked in and asked to see the president of the bank. He came out and asked me into his office. I presented the check and asked him to wire the funds to my bank in Texas.

I will always remember his face. He turned white as a ghost. He walked to the back of the bank and talked with another couple of bankers. His problem was that the auctioneer, Dave, was still in Texas (with the checks from the auction). The president came back into his office and explained that Dave did not have $1 million dollars in his account "just right" now. I presented the president with his own letter that guaranteed any check Dave wrote.

The president turned a whiter shade of white, if that is possible. After conferring with his staff for forty five minutes, he agreed to wire the funds to my bank in Texas. Before I left the premises, I confirmed that the money had arrived. Strangely, I did not seem to be welcome as I waited in the Little Rock bank that day.

After I returned, I got a hot phone call from Dave, the auctioneer. I will not print the language he used here. I got a similar call from Bob a few days later. He called me many names which I will also not print here.

If they had been gentlemen with me in the process, I would have been a gentleman with them. It was my responsibility to collect that $1 million and I was going to do it. My bank was paid in full and I was satisfied with that.

I suspect that was the last letter that the Little Rock bank president wrote guaranteeing any check that a client would write.

— R. STUBLER —

Chapter 22

The Scout

I will always remember when I turned sixteen years old. For a young man in Oklahoma in January 1972, it was a significant event. I got my driver's license. Getting my driver's license meant two significant things: to be able to go hunting on my own and to be able to take out girls.

I had been dating a young redhead I will call Dee (just to be safe). She was as sweet as could be and I had been riding my bike over to her house to see her. Most of the boys in my class already had their driver's licenses and many of them already had their own cars.

I tell you, it is hard to be cool when you are nearly sixteen and riding a bike to pick up your date. Obviously, we could not go anywhere, so we just watched TV, talked, and went on walks.

In January, I got my license to drive. A couple of weeks later, I talked my father into borrowing his 1964 International Scout pickup on Saturday evening. I went to pick up Dee and took her out to the lake to watch submarine races. Watching submarine races meant driving out to Lake Atoka and looking at big limbs sticking up in the water. If you watched them closely when there was a wind, the limb looked a little like a periscope on submarine moving through the water. I know this sounds weak, but that was the story we told girls when we were driving them to the lake to try to "make out."

The Scout was not much of a vehicle. It would run, but very slowly. Once I managed to get it up to sixty-five miles an hour on a long downhill run but that was max speed. Normally, it would only go about forty-five miles per hour, which was probably a good thing if you knew me. It also was two wheel drive and the tires were nearly bald.

I thought the Scout would go anywhere. I had a friend who had a Scout that would climb hills and buzz through mud holes. Of course, his was four wheel drive and had great tires.

Back to the lake, I know you want to know more. Dee and I watched the submarines for a while and then I decided to take her up the lake trail. I had previously been there with my friend's Scout so I thought Dad's Scout could make it.

Going up the mountain trail by the lake was fairly easy; we did not have any problems. When we came down the mountain, I was pulling the Scout up to the main road when we got stuck.

I was not happy. Here we were at 10:30 in the evening, stuck by the side of the road. I knew there was a house about a mile away. We could walk to the house, call my father, and he would come out and get us out of the ditch we were in. However, my father did not know we were at the lake and I was not eager to call him.

For forty five minutes, I tried everything I could think of to get the Scout out of the ditch. Nothing worked.

Thirty minutes later, a car drove by, saw us, and stopped. Out of the car came four drunk guys. I was worried. At sixteen, I was about 5'6" tall and weighed about 145 pounds and these were big guys in their twenties.

I talked to the leader, he laughed and asked me what my problem was. I told him that we were stuck and he said he would be glad to help. I got out a rope, we tied it to the Scout, and we were out in a couple of minutes.

While Dee waited in the Scout, I walked up to the guys. I thanked them and then pulled out my wallet to give them some money. I had a total of three dollars in my wallet.

The leader of the guys looked in my wallet as I pulled out the three dollars and burst out laughing. He said, "Son, I have seen your date and you need all the money you have to spend on that nice girl." With that, he laughed louder, put his crew in his car and left.

That spring, my father took me to a place to hunt squirrels where he had hunted when he was a boy. It was about five miles south out of town and was a huge river bottom that was full of squirrels.

Now that I had been driving the Scout on weekends to hunt and to date, I was working on my father to take off the top of the Scout. It had a simple top that could be removed simply by taking off sixteen bolts.

Dad was not receptive to taking off the top. Safety was always a concern with my father. But, being a typical teenage boy, I worked on him on this issue every day. He continued to tell me no, but I continued to ask. One Friday, I finally got him 98% the way there to letting me take off the top. I could just see myself riding around in the Scout without that top. Man, young ladies would not be able to resist me, I thought. But Dad regrouped and continued to say no to taking off the top.

The next day, I got up early to go squirrel hunting. I drove to Cousin John's house and picked him up. He and I were best friends, and he was a great hunting partner. We also took along his younger brothers, David and Brian.

We drove down the country road on our way to a big bottom south of town. It was about an hour before daylight and very dark. The Scout's headlights were dim, nothing like the lights on our vehicles today. As I drove down the road, the road made a slight left curve and I did not curve with it.

I was probably only going about fifteen miles an hour but that was fast enough to cause a problem. As I tried to correct by turning left, we began to slip into the ditch on our right.

The ditch turned into a hole and I flipped the Scout completely upside down. Since I was small for my age, I remained in the same position through the spin; the Scout turned upside down but I remained in a death grip on the steering wheel so I ended up sitting upright upside down now on the roof of the Scout. The Scout was upside down, lying on its roof, with all four tires in the air. The hole was so big that you could barely see the top of the Scout's tires looking from the road.

So, here we were. Four boys, ages 16, 14, 12, and 10, in an up-side down Scout in a hole on the side of a country road. To say we were dazed would be a major understatement.

After about thirty seconds, John said to me, "Well, turn the engine off at least." The Scout's motor was still running. It was a small motor and you could barely hear it humming along (upside down).

We walked to a farmhouse and called our fathers. They were relieved that none of us had so much as a scratch so they took the news better than we feared.

Our fathers came out with a friend who had a wrecker service. He winched the Scout out and you could barely tell that anything had happened. The roof was a little caved in but we simply kicked it back out and it looked virtually the same as before. The hole where we landed was muddy and that, plus the low speed, saved the Scout and us from damage.

Dad would never consider taking the top off the Scout after that and who was I to argue with the man? He reminded me that he was right about this for over forty years. The man just loved being right.

Chapter 23

ATM Cash

In 1998, I was working at a bank in Plano, Texas. My boss called me into his office and told me he wanted me to meet with Jim Books. Jim had an unusual request and my boss thought I was the perfect guy to talk with him since I had a background in lending and operations.

Jim Books was a current customer of the bank. He had grown up in Plano and was like a son to one of our directors.

Jim owned two companies. One was an armored car company but his main company was an ATM company. He placed ATMs in convenience stores in Texas, Arizona, and Colorado.

At the time I met with Jim, the bank had a couple of small loans to his ATM company totaling less than $125,000.

I sat down with Jim and he explained the nature of his request. He had over eighty ATMs and had to keep cash in the machines. He had an arrangement with two banks in Colorado where the banks were providing him over $4,000,000 in cash to stock his ATMs.

At first, I thought that the Colorado banks were loaning him the $4 million to stock his ATMs. But he said no, they were only supplying the cash. I was confused.

Jim explained that the cash was owned by the banks and was shown on their balance sheets as vault cash. This made no sense to me but I listened to his further explanation.

He said the Colorado banks were able to show that the cash was still in their control because the cash was in control of the bonded armored car company. He said the accounting had been approved by the banks' regulator and that he could get me a copy of that opinion.

I asked him why he wanted my bank to start providing him cash if he already had banks providing it.

He said the banks kept increasing the cost of providing the cash even though they were happy to have the business. The cost was currently $4,000 dollars a month and he wanted to reduce that cost. I took the billing information from the other banks back to my office to give it some study.

After I had looked at the information for some time, my boss came into my office. After hearing the details, my boss was fired up to do the deal. He said we could charge Jim $3,000 a month and that $36,000 a year income would greatly help our cost center.

I looked at my boss and said that I could not see how I could recommend that our bank take this over. I said this arrangement made no sense to me.

My boss said, "Mixon, you are not getting it. Our bank is going to make $36,000 a year with almost no risk." Plus, he reminded me, Jim was well known and respected at our bank.

"We have complete faith in Jim," he added.

We had a long discussion. He criticized me for not thinking "outside of the box."

I told him that I could not figure out how to make the risk equal the return. What Jim was proposing was having his companies have complete access and control to $4 million of the bank's cash. I could not calculate the return the bank would need in order to take on that risk.

My boss asked me if I was smarter than these Colorado banks. I said I did not know but the deal just did not make any sense to me.

My boss was not happy with me (and later included this on my review). But we turned down the request.

Two years later, Jim disappeared with the money. He reappeared in a few months and was arrested.

In 2002, Jim was found guilty of 46 counts of bank fraud, wire fraud and money laundering. He was sentenced to nearly six years in prison for defrauding two Colorado banks of about $9 million and ordered to pay $9.2 million in restitution to the FDIC.

I was, obviously, very happy that I did not put our bank in a position to lose $4 million. I do not know how this scam grew from $4 million to $9 million but I was relieved that our bank had no part in it.

-R.STUBLER-

Chapter 24

Skipping School

In April 1972, I was sixteen and a sophomore in Atoka High School. The winter had been a cold one and one afternoon it warmed up to 75 degrees.

Being a Mixon, I started thinking about fishing when a little warm weather popped up. I approached my friend George at lunch and proposed that he and I leave school after lunch and head to a fishing hole that I knew.

George had never fished much but he too was tempted by the prospect of getting out in the sun. George told me that he could not go. I asked why but I knew the answer. George was terrified of his father. His father was a Colonel in the Air Force and was an imposing figure: six foot two inches and not an ounce of fat on him. He was one tough father.

I reminded George that his father was out of town and began to work on wearing him down.

George was worried about his grades. What if skipping two classes would affect his grades, he wondered. I reminded George that he and I both had A averages and that neither of us had any tests in our two afternoon classes that day.

After much debate, George agreed to go with me. We got into the Scout and headed out to a fishing hole after picking up our fishing equipment at our houses.

What a beautiful day it was! The sun was shining and the air was filled with a wonderful springtime smell. The fish were not biting but it was a great afternoon. It was the kind of day that made you feel great to be alive.

After a couple of hours, I suggested that we take a swim. George told me that I was crazy. I told George that I had been swimming in the hole many times at this time of year and that it would be warmer than he thought. (An absolute lie).

Surprisingly, he believed me. We both stripped down to our undies and prepared to jump off a five foot cliff into the water.

In the past, I had been swimming in this fishing hole and knew the water was deep enough for this jump. We agreed to run and jump together at the count of five.

We counted to five and ran toward the cliff. George jumped and I stayed on the cliff. (I have to tell it like it happened. Never trust a Mixon in a counting game.)

George hit the water. Let's just say it was a tad colder than he expected. You could have heard him holler for a good mile. I am ashamed to say that I was on the cliff laughing my head off.

George got out and was an exceptionally good friend for not holding this against me. He joined me in my laughter while his teeth were chattering – it had been a cold winter and the water was probably about 60 degrees.

We decided to head home. I drove to George's house and we pulled up at 3:30, just about the time school was letting out. George was carrying his fishing rods and I was carrying his tackle box.

We stepped into his house. Just as we entered the house, George's father stepped out. I will always remember his face, hard as stone. I thought George was going to pass out. It was obvious that we had been skipping school (the fishing equipment) and George's father was not happy.

George's father turned to me and said, "Mixon, you can go."

I felt so sorry for George, but I wheeled on my feet and slipped right on out of there.

That evening, George's father called my father and told him what had happened and that I was a bad influence on George. George's father added that he was grounding George for six months and suggested my father should do the same with me.

Dad got off the phone and asked "How are your grades?" I told him that I still had an A average. Then he asked me if we caught any fish. I told him no. He laughed and that was the end of it.

Poor George was grounded for six months and his father was very hard on him over this. George later told me that that day was worth it. And it was. I was lucky to have a father that recognized what was important in a young man's life – one day of skipping school and enjoying the outdoors.

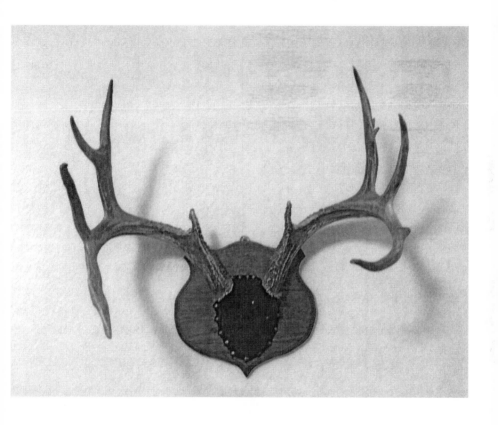

Chapter 25

Old One Shot

I am sitting here looking at a huge set of whitetail deer antlers. They are on the wall in my office and measure twenty inches on the inside, heavy antlers with twelve points. Working at a bank in Texas, I will be talking to a fellow about a loan when

154 | *Texas Banker/Oklahoma Hunter: A Mostly True Story*

he will notice the antlers. He will stop mid-sentence and stare at the antlers. (I always know a hunter when I see one). He will offer a compliment and ask me where I killed the buck. I answer that that buck got completely away from me. The fellow will look puzzled and ask me what I mean. That, dear friends, is the Rest of the Story.

In 1971, my father, my sister's husband Dan, and I decided to build a tree stand on the Atoka Game Reserve. We picked out a huge oak tree at the top of a big hill. My father can take things to excess on occasion, and we built this huge stand about twenty feet up in this tree. Three grown men could sit side by side in the stand. It wasn't fancy but it sure was sturdy.

My father really should have been a safety engineer. He worked forty-three years for Southwestern Bell and had only one accident in that time, as he would proudly tell you. We built that tree stand strong and sturdy and you could see about a half mile in three directions. You could have put a refrigerator on top of that stand and it would not have given an inch.

It was about an hour before daybreak when Dad, Dan, and I started for the tree stand. I was fifteen and so excited I was ready to run the mile to the stand. Dan and I took our positions in the stand; Dan on the upper limb and me on the main seat in the stand. Dad was making a circle as usual. (Dad rarely sat on a stand. Said he hunted better on foot. I think he simply could not sit still very long in the cold.)

About thirty minutes after sunup, Dan said, "Oh my gawd, there he is!" I looked down the hill. There was a huge buck at the bottom of the hill, just standing there with the sun shining off his antlers. I can still see him in my mind today. Even at three hundred yards, he looked like an elk. He was huge. I was carrying a borrowed .270 and I quickly found him in my scope. But Dan was faster and fired his .30-06 just as I let the safety off.

I am sure it sounded like a war as Dan and I fired three shots apiece at the buck. There were some rocky cliffs to the left of the buck and I noticed the sound of the shots echoing off the rocks. The buck thought the shots were coming from there and turned and ran straight up the hill toward us. I would like to tell you I was calm and cool as the buck charged toward me. But I would be a liar. I pulled down on the buck and waited for him to get to a clearing.

As the buck entered the clearing, I squeezed the trigger. Snap! That .270 was difficult in loading shells and I had made an error in putting the shells too far back, causing the hammer to strike the shell with too little force to fire. I jerked back on the bolt and rammed it forward. I had jammed a shell sideways in the gun and it was stuck there. I sat there helplessly as the buck ran within fifty yards of the tree and out of sight over the hill.

Dan climbed out of the tree and took out after him. I sat in the tree yelling at that gun and trying to get the shell out of it. Dad walked up to the tree in about fifteen minutes. "What the heck is all the shooting and yelling about," Dad asked. I told him the story as I got down from the tree. He asked if we hit the buck. I told him it was unlikely, but that I was going to walk over and see if there was any blood. I traded him the .270 for the .30-30 pump rifle that he was carrying. It had a habit of jamming too, but I did not want anything to do with the .270. I tore off after Dan.

About thirty minutes later, I was over the hill about two hundred yards when I heard a single shot. I immediately knew
it was Dad. I hustled back to the stand. As I walked up to the
tree, he was climbing down.

"Ken, I got him, I got him," Dad declared. We walked down
the hill together and found the dead buck. Dad told me he
had seen the buck sneaking through the woods behind him
down the hill. He finally got a clear shot at one hundred and
fifty yards. That son-of-a-gun buck had circled and was headed back from where he came from when Dad ambushed him.
Killed him with one shot, no less.

The buck dressed out at 150 pounds and won the county Big
Buck contest that year. Dad won a fine Remington semi-auto
.30-06 which he hunted with for the remainder of his life. Dad
called himself Old One Shot for the rest of his days.

Dad gave me the antlers in 1993. I am proud to have them in
my office. But I tell you, if my gun hadn't jammed, I would

have got that buck. But he got clean away.

Well, from me, anyway.

Final Chapter

DAD 6/2/15

What can I say about my Father?

He was my Best Friend.

He taught me to play basketball.

He taught me about life.

He taught me to hunt.

I remember when I was ten and he took me to the woods.

We hunted squirrel for a couple of hours in Boggy Bottom.

When we finished, he asked me to find the way back.

We walked and walked but I could not find the way out.

He led me out of the woods.

He said, "You need to be able to find your way home."

Ever since then, I have kept this in my mind.

You need to be able to find your way home.

Growing up we always had dogs.

Two were very special to my father.

Lady was half English Pointer and half Brittany Spaniel.

She was the sweetest dog and had a real knack for finding quail.

After Lady died, we got Charlie, a big boned English Setter.

Hardheaded, man, he was hardheaded.

But Dad finally got him to "whoa" after some lessons with a rope.

Charlie could find birds but Charlie would only hunt for Dad.

When I took Charlie hunting by myself, he would just play.

He knew I was not Boss.

Dad was.

As I got older, Dad would take me deer hunting with him.

Often we would be walking along hunting and be 75 yards or

so apart.

If Dad wanted to know where I was, he had a special whistle.

It was just two long tones, one high tone followed by one low-

er tone.

It meant where are you?

My job was to whistle back with the same two tones.

This meant I am right here and I am OK.

Over the years, I would be hunting, maybe in a tree stand.

I would be sitting there, watching the woods.

Then I would hear his familiar whistle and know

Everything was right in my world.

Today when I hunt with my son,

I use that same whistle to see where he is.

He whistles back to tell me he is fine.

Then I know everything is right in my world.

So now that Dad is gone, I have these images in my mind.

One is Dad sitting around a campfire with his father and family.

They will be telling stories about the old days.

Stories of hunting quail.

Stories about great football teams.

Deer hunting tales.

Stories about their sons and daughters.

Stories about their grandchildren and great grandchildren.

Each trying to out story the other.

The next picture I have of my father is him hunting in heaven.

He will be quail hunting, you see, with his old sixteen gauge.

Lady will be with him, hunting close.

Charlie will be there too, out ranging where he can find the birds.

Dad will be grinning his big grin

Because he has the best two quail dogs in heaven.

The last image I have is the best.

This is the day when I cross over.

I will be there, at the edge of a big, beautiful, green forest.

There will be a beautiful stream running through the middle of the forest.

I won't know exactly what to do.

Birds are singing and the smallmouth bass are jumping.

As I take this all in, I hear this whistle.

Two long tones.

There he will be.

Grinning as only my father can.

He will put his arm around me.

He will say "I am glad you found your way home."

About the Author

Ken Mixon was born in Ardmore, Oklahoma in 1956. He is the son of Jim Mixon and Bonnie Jean Mixon. He has one sister, Sandra Lee Grace.

He married Martha Carol Efurd in December 1977. He has two children, Beth Killian and Drew Mixon. Beth has two children, Faith Caroline Qualls and Tyler Lynn Killian. Drew and his wife, Jemima Clayden Mixon, have two children, Lyla Bonnie Mixon and Kenny Lee Mixon.

Ken was raised in Atoka, Oklahoma and graduated from Atoka High School in 1974. He attended Oklahoma Baptist University and graduated in 1977 with a degree in business administration.

In 1977, he started his banking career as an auditor with First

National Bank in Oklahoma City. He worked as a teller and other positions in banks in Oklahoma before moving to Texas in 1982. At that time, he became Cashier and Chief Financial Officer at First City Bank, Gate-

way in Beaumont, Texas. In 1985, he returned to Oklahoma to work for a couple of years at a bank in central Oklahoma.

In 1987, he moved back to Texas for good when he accepted a position with First City Bank in Richardson. In 1989, he became President of First City Bank in Garland. From 1994 to 2012, he worked at a number of Dallas area banks. In 2012, he became President and CEO of City National Bank in Corsicana, where he remains today.

Ken is a member of First Baptist Church in Richardson and is very proud to be a Rotary member in Corsicana. One of his biggest passions is being involved in selecting the high school senior to receive the Corsicana Rotary Scholarship each year.

Ken is a big fan of the Dallas Mavericks, Dallas Cowboys, and Oklahoma Sooners. He enjoys hunting and fishing and being with family and friends.

About the Illustrator

Richard Stubler has been drawing cartoons for fifty years. He currently lives in Orlando, Florida. His work has appeared in various magazines across America. His book, Hunting and Fishing Cartoons, is available at rstubler@cfl.rr.com.

CPSIA information can be obtained
at www.ICGtesting.com
Printed in the USA
FFOW04n1928291116

9 780692 760987